Globalization: A Very Short Introduction

VERY SHORT INTRODUCTIONS are for anyone wanting a stimulating and accessible way in to a new subject. They are written by experts and have been translated into more than 40 different languages. The series began in 1995 and now covers a wide variety of topics in every discipline. The VSI library contains nearly 400 volumes—a Very Short Introduction to everything from Indian philosophy to psychology and American history—and continues to grow in every subject area.

Very Short Introductions available now:

ACCOUNTING Christopher Nobes
ADVERTISING Winston Fletcher
AFRICAN HISTORY John Parker and Richard Rathbone
AGNOSTICISM Robin Le Poidevin
ALEXANDER THE GREAT Hugh Bowden
AMERICAN HISTORY Paul S. Boyer
AMERICAN IMMIGRATION David A. Gerber
AMERICAN POLITICAL PARTIES AND ELECTIONS L. Sandy Maisel
AMERICAN POLITICS Richard M. Valelly
THE AMERICAN PRESIDENCY Charles O. Jones
ANAESTHESIA Aidan O'Donnell
ANARCHISM Colin Ward
ANCIENT EGYPT Ian Shaw
ANCIENT GREECE Paul Cartledge
THE ANCIENT NEAR EAST Amanda H. Podany
ANCIENT PHILOSOPHY Julia Annas
ANCIENT WARFARE Harry Sidebottom
ANGELS David Albert Jones
ANGLICANISM Mark Chapman
THE ANGLO-SAXON AGE John Blair
THE ANIMAL KINGDOM Peter Holland
ANIMAL RIGHTS David DeGrazia
THE ANTARCTIC Klaus Dodds
ANTISEMITISM Steven Beller
ANXIETY Daniel Freeman and Jason Freeman
THE APOCRYPHAL GOSPELS Paul Foster
ARCHAEOLOGY Paul Bahn
ARCHITECTURE Andrew Ballantyne
ARISTOCRACY William Doyle
ARISTOTLE Jonathan Barnes
ART HISTORY Dana Arnold
ART THEORY Cynthia Freeland
ASTROBIOLOGY David C. Catling
ATHEISM Julian Baggini
AUGUSTINE Henry Chadwick
AUSTRALIA Kenneth Morgan
AUTISM Uta Frith
THE AVANT GARDE David Cottington
THE AZTECS Davíd Carrasco
BACTERIA Sebastian G. B. Amyes
BARTHES Jonathan Culler
THE BEATS David Sterritt
BEAUTY Roger Scruton
BESTSELLERS John Sutherland
THE BIBLE John Riches
BIBLICAL ARCHAEOLOGY Eric H. Cline
BIOGRAPHY Hermione Lee
THE BLUES Elijah Wald
THE BOOK OF MORMON Terryl Givens
BORDERS Alexander C. Diener and Joshua Hagen
THE BRAIN Michael O'Shea
THE BRITISH CONSTITUTION Martin Loughlin
THE BRITISH EMPIRE Ashley Jackson
BRITISH POLITICS Anthony Wright
BUDDHA Michael Carrithers
BUDDHISM Damien Keown
BUDDHIST ETHICS Damien Keown
CANCER Nicholas James
CAPITALISM James Fulcher
CATHOLICISM Gerald O'Collins

CAUSATION Stephen Mumford and Rani Lill Anjum
THE CELL Terence Allen and Graham Cowling
THE CELTS Barry Cunliffe
CHAOS Leonard Smith
CHILDREN'S LITERATURE Kimberley Reynolds
CHINESE LITERATURE Sabina Knight
CHOICE THEORY Michael Allingham
CHRISTIAN ART Beth Williamson
CHRISTIAN ETHICS D. Stephen Long
CHRISTIANITY Linda Woodhead
CITIZENSHIP Richard Bellamy
CIVIL ENGINEERING David Muir Wood
CLASSICAL LITERATURE William Allan
CLASSICAL MYTHOLOGY Helen Morales
CLASSICS Mary Beard and John Henderson
CLAUSEWITZ Michael Howard
CLIMATE Mark Maslin
THE COLD WAR Robert McMahon
COLONIAL AMERICA Alan Taylor
COLONIAL LATIN AMERICAN LITERATURE Rolena Adorno
COMEDY Matthew Bevis
COMMUNISM Leslie Holmes
COMPLEXITY John H. Holland
THE COMPUTER Darrel Ince
THE CONQUISTADORS Matthew Restall and Felipe Fernández-Armesto
CONSCIENCE Paul Strohm
CONSCIOUSNESS Susan Blackmore
CONTEMPORARY ART Julian Stallabrass
CONTEMPORARY FICTION Robert Eaglestone
CONTINENTAL PHILOSOPHY Simon Critchley
CORAL REEFS Charles Sheppard
COSMOLOGY Peter Coles
CRITICAL THEORY Stephen Eric Bronner
THE CRUSADES Christopher Tyerman
CRYPTOGRAPHY Fred Piper and Sean Murphy
THE CULTURAL REVOLUTION Richard Curt Kraus
DADA AND SURREALISM David Hopkins
DARWIN Jonathan Howard
THE DEAD SEA SCROLLS Timothy Lim
DEMOCRACY Bernard Crick
DERRIDA Simon Glendinning
DESCARTES Tom Sorell
DESERTS Nick Middleton
DESIGN John Heskett
DEVELOPMENTAL BIOLOGY Lewis Wolpert
THE DEVIL Darren Oldridge
DIASPORA Kevin Kenny
DICTIONARIES Lynda Mugglestone
DINOSAURS David Norman
DIPLOMACY Joseph M. Siracusa
DOCUMENTARY FILM Patricia Aufderheide
DREAMING J. Allan Hobson
DRUGS Leslie Iversen
DRUIDS Barry Cunliffe
EARLY MUSIC Thomas Forrest Kelly
THE EARTH Martin Redfern
ECONOMICS Partha Dasgupta
EDUCATION Gary Thomas
EGYPTIAN MYTH Geraldine Pinch
EIGHTEENTH-CENTURY BRITAIN Paul Langford
THE ELEMENTS Philip Ball
EMOTION Dylan Evans
EMPIRE Stephen Howe
ENGELS Terrell Carver
ENGINEERING David Blockley
ENGLISH LITERATURE Jonathan Bate
ENVIRONMENTAL ECONOMICS Stephen Smith
EPIDEMIOLOGY Rodolfo Saracci
ETHICS Simon Blackburn
THE EUROPEAN UNION John Pinder and Simon Usherwood
EVOLUTION Brian and Deborah Charlesworth
EXISTENTIALISM Thomas Flynn
THE EYE Michael Land
FAMILY LAW Jonathan Herring
FASCISM Kevin Passmore
FASHION Rebecca Arnold
FEMINISM Margaret Walters
FILM Michael Wood
FILM MUSIC Kathryn Kalinak
THE FIRST WORLD WAR Michael Howard
FOLK MUSIC Mark Slobin
FOOD John Krebs
FORENSIC PSYCHOLOGY David Canter
FORENSIC SCIENCE Jim Fraser
FOSSILS Keith Thomson

FOUCAULT Gary Gutting
FRACTALS Kenneth Falconer
FREE SPEECH Nigel Warburton
FREE WILL Thomas Pink
FRENCH LITERATURE John D. Lyons
THE FRENCH REVOLUTION William Doyle
FREUD Anthony Storr
FUNDAMENTALISM Malise Ruthven
GALAXIES John Gribbin
GALILEO Stillman Drake
GAME THEORY Ken Binmore
GANDHI Bhikhu Parekh
GENIUS Andrew Robinson
GEOGRAPHY John Matthews and David Herbert
GEOPOLITICS Klaus Dodds
GERMAN LITERATURE Nicholas Boyle
GERMAN PHILOSOPHY Andrew Bowie
GLOBAL CATASTROPHES Bill McGuire
GLOBAL ECONOMIC HISTORY Robert C. Allen
GLOBAL WARMING Mark Maslin
GLOBALIZATION Manfred Steger
THE GOTHIC Nick Groom
GOVERNANCE Mark Bevir
THE GREAT DEPRESSION AND THE NEW DEAL Eric Rauchway
HABERMAS James Gordon Finlayson
HAPPINESS Daniel M. Haybron
HEGEL Peter Singer
HEIDEGGER Michael Inwood
HERODOTUS Jennifer T. Roberts
HIEROGLYPHS Penelope Wilson
HINDUISM Kim Knott
HISTORY John H. Arnold
THE HISTORY OF ASTRONOMY Michael Hoskin
THE HISTORY OF LIFE Michael Benton
THE HISTORY OF MATHEMATICS Jacqueline Stedall
THE HISTORY OF MEDICINE William Bynum
THE HISTORY OF TIME Leofranc Holford-Strevens
HIV/AIDS Alan Whiteside
HOBBES Richard Tuck
HORMONES Martin Luck
HUMAN EVOLUTION Bernard Wood
HUMAN RIGHTS Andrew Clapham
HUMANISM Stephen Law
HUME A. J. Ayer
HUMOUR Noël Carroll
THE ICE AGE Jamie Woodward
IDEOLOGY Michael Freeden
INDIAN PHILOSOPHY Sue Hamilton
INFORMATION Luciano Floridi
INNOVATION Mark Dodgson and David Gann
INTELLIGENCE Ian J. Deary
INTERNATIONAL MIGRATION Khalid Koser
INTERNATIONAL RELATIONS Paul Wilkinson
INTERNATIONAL SECURITY Christopher S. Browning
ISLAM Malise Ruthven
ISLAMIC HISTORY Adam Silverstein
ITALIAN LITERATURE Peter Hainsworth and David Robey
JESUS Richard Bauckham
JOURNALISM Ian Hargreaves
JUDAISM Norman Solomon
JUNG Anthony Stevens
KABBALAH Joseph Dan
KAFKA Ritchie Robertson
KANT Roger Scruton
KEYNES Robert Skidelsky
KIERKEGAARD Patrick Gardiner
THE KORAN Michael Cook
LANDSCAPE ARCHITECTURE Ian H. Thompson
LANDSCAPES AND GEOMORPHOLOGY Andrew Goudie and Heather Viles
LANGUAGES Stephen R. Anderson
LATE ANTIQUITY Gillian Clark
LAW Raymond Wacks
THE LAWS OF THERMODYNAMICS Peter Atkins
LEADERSHIP Keith Grint
LINCOLN Allen C. Guelzo
LINGUISTICS Peter Matthews
LITERARY THEORY Jonathan Culler
LOCKE John Dunn
LOGIC Graham Priest
MACHIAVELLI Quentin Skinner
MADNESS Andrew Scull
MAGIC Owen Davies
MAGNA CARTA Nicholas Vincent

MAGNETISM Stephen Blundell
MALTHUS Donald Winch
MANAGEMENT John Hendry
MAO Delia Davin
MARINE BIOLOGY Philip V. Mladenov
THE MARQUIS DE SADE John Phillips
MARTIN LUTHER Scott H. Hendrix
MARTYRDOM Jolyon Mitchell
MARX Peter Singer
MATHEMATICS Timothy Gowers
THE MEANING OF LIFE Terry Eagleton
MEDICAL ETHICS Tony Hope
MEDICAL LAW Charles Foster
MEDIEVAL BRITAIN John Gillingham and Ralph A. Griffiths
MEMORY Jonathan K. Foster
METAPHYSICS Stephen Mumford
MICHAEL FARADAY Frank A.J.L. James
MICROECONOMICS Avinash Dixit
MODERN ART David Cottington
MODERN CHINA Rana Mitter
MODERN FRANCE Vanessa R. Schwartz
MODERN IRELAND Senia Pašeta
MODERN JAPAN Christopher Goto-Jones
MODERN LATIN AMERICAN LITERATURE Roberto González Echevarría
MODERN WAR Richard English
MODERNISM Christopher Butler
MOLECULES Philip Ball
THE MONGOLS Morris Rossabi
MORMONISM Richard Lyman Bushman
MUHAMMAD Jonathan A.C. Brown
MULTICULTURALISM Ali Rattansi
MUSIC Nicholas Cook
MYTH Robert A. Segal
THE NAPOLEONIC WARS Mike Rapport
NATIONALISM Steven Grosby
NELSON MANDELA Elleke Boehmer
NEOLIBERALISM Manfred Steger and Ravi Roy
NETWORKS Guido Caldarelli and Michele Catanzaro
THE NEW TESTAMENT Luke Timothy Johnson
THE NEW TESTAMENT AS LITERATURE Kyle Keefer
NEWTON Robert Iliffe
NIETZSCHE Michael Tanner
NINETEENTH-CENTURY BRITAIN Christopher Harvie and H. C. G. Matthew
THE NORMAN CONQUEST George Garnett
NORTH AMERICAN INDIANS Theda Perdue and Michael D. Green
NORTHERN IRELAND Marc Mulholland
NOTHING Frank Close
NUCLEAR POWER Maxwell Irvine
NUCLEAR WEAPONS Joseph M. Siracusa
NUMBERS Peter M. Higgins
NUTRITION David A. Bender
OBJECTIVITY Stephen Gaukroger
THE OLD TESTAMENT Michael D. Coogan
THE ORCHESTRA D. Kern Holoman
ORGANIZATIONS Mary Jo Hatch
PAGANISM Owen Davies
THE PALESTINIAN-ISRAELI CONFLICT Martin Bunton
PARTICLE PHYSICS Frank Close
PAUL E. P. Sanders
PENTECOSTALISM William K. Kay
THE PERIODIC TABLE Eric R. Scerri
PHILOSOPHY Edward Craig
PHILOSOPHY OF LAW Raymond Wacks
PHILOSOPHY OF SCIENCE Samir Okasha
PHOTOGRAPHY Steve Edwards
PLAGUE Paul Slack
PLANETS David A. Rothery
PLANTS Timothy Walker
PLATO Julia Annas
POLITICAL PHILOSOPHY David Miller
POLITICS Kenneth Minogue
POSTCOLONIALISM Robert Young
POSTMODERNISM Christopher Butler
POSTSTRUCTURALISM Catherine Belsey
PREHISTORY Chris Gosden
PRESOCRATIC PHILOSOPHY Catherine Osborne
PRIVACY Raymond Wacks
PROBABILITY John Haigh
PROGRESSIVISM Walter Nugent
PROTESTANTISM Mark A. Noll

PSYCHIATRY Tom Burns
PSYCHOLOGY Gillian Butler and Freda McManus
PURITANISM Francis J. Bremer
THE QUAKERS Pink Dandelion
QUANTUM THEORY John Polkinghorne
RACISM Ali Rattansi
RADIOACTIVITY Claudio Tuniz
RASTAFARI Ennis B. Edmonds
THE REAGAN REVOLUTION Gil Troy
REALITY Jan Westerhoff
THE REFORMATION Peter Marshall
RELATIVITY Russell Stannard
RELIGION IN AMERICA Timothy Beal
THE RENAISSANCE Jerry Brotton
RENAISSANCE ART Geraldine A. Johnson
REVOLUTIONS Jack A. Goldstone
RHETORIC Richard Toye
RISK Baruch Fischhoff and John Kadvany
RIVERS Nick Middleton
ROBOTICS Alan Winfield
ROMAN BRITAIN Peter Salway
THE ROMAN EMPIRE Christopher Kelly
THE ROMAN REPUBLIC David M. Gwynn
ROMANTICISM Michael Ferber
ROUSSEAU Robert Wokler
RUSSELL A. C. Grayling
RUSSIAN HISTORY Geoffrey Hosking
RUSSIAN LITERATURE Catriona Kelly
THE RUSSIAN REVOLUTION S. A. Smith
SCHIZOPHRENIA Chris Frith and Eve Johnstone
SCHOPENHAUER Christopher Janaway
SCIENCE AND RELIGION Thomas Dixon
SCIENCE FICTION David Seed
THE SCIENTIFIC REVOLUTION Lawrence M. Principe
SCOTLAND Rab Houston
SEXUALITY Véronique Mottier
SHAKESPEARE Germaine Greer
SIKHISM Eleanor Nesbitt
THE SILK ROAD James A. Millward
SLEEP Steven W. Lockley and Russell G. Foster
SOCIAL AND CULTURAL ANTHROPOLOGY John Monaghan and Peter Just
SOCIALISM Michael Newman
SOCIOLINGUISTICS John Edwards
SOCIOLOGY Steve Bruce
SOCRATES C. C. W. Taylor
THE SOVIET UNION Stephen Lovell
THE SPANISH CIVIL WAR Helen Graham
SPANISH LITERATURE Jo Labanyi
SPINOZA Roger Scruton
SPIRITUALITY Philip Sheldrake
STARS Andrew King
STATISTICS David J. Hand
STEM CELLS Jonathan Slack
STUART BRITAIN John Morrill
SUPERCONDUCTIVITY Stephen Blundell
SYMMETRY Ian Stewart
TEETH Peter S. Ungar
TERRORISM Charles Townshend
THEOLOGY David F. Ford
THOMAS AQUINAS Fergus Kerr
THOUGHT Tim Bayne
TIBETAN BUDDHISM Matthew T. Kapstein
TOCQUEVILLE Harvey C. Mansfield
TRAGEDY Adrian Poole
THE TROJAN WAR Eric H. Cline
TRUST Katherine Hawley
THE TUDORS John Guy
TWENTIETH-CENTURY BRITAIN Kenneth O. Morgan
THE UNITED NATIONS Jussi M. Hanhimäki
THE U.S. CONGRESS Donald A. Ritchie
THE U.S. SUPREME COURT Linda Greenhouse
UTOPIANISM Lyman Tower Sargent
THE VIKINGS Julian Richards
VIRUSES Dorothy H. Crawford
WITCHCRAFT Malcolm Gaskill
WITTGENSTEIN A. C. Grayling
WORK Stephen Fineman
WORLD MUSIC Philip Bohlman
THE WORLD TRADE ORGANIZATION Amrita Narlikar
WRITING AND SCRIPT Andrew Robinson

Manfred B. Steger

GLOBALIZATION

A Very Short Introduction

OXFORD
UNIVERSITY PRESS

OXFORD
UNIVERSITY PRESS

Great Clarendon Street, Oxford, OX2 6DP,
United Kingdom

Oxford University Press is a department of the University of Oxford. It furthers the University's objective of excellence in research, scholarship, and education by publishing worldwide. Oxford is a registered trade mark of Oxford University Press in the UK and in certain other countries

First Edition published in 2003
Second Edition published in 2009
This Edition published 2013

Impression: 5

British Library Cataloguing in Publication Data
Data available

ISBN 978-0-19-966266-1

Printed in Great Britain by
Ashford Colour Press Ltd, Gosport, Hampshire

Contents

Preface to the third edition xi

List of abbreviations xv

List of illustrations xvii

List of maps xix

List of figures xxi

1 Globalization: a contested concept 1

2 Globalization and history: is globalization a new phenomenon? 17

3 The economic dimension of globalization 37

4 The political dimension of globalization 60

5 The cultural dimension of globalization 74

6 The ecological dimension of globalization 87

7 Ideologies of globalization: market globalism, justice globalism, religious globalisms 103

8 Global crises and the future of globalization 131

References 139

Index 147

Preface to the third edition

It is a gratifying experience to present readers with the third edition of this introduction to globalization that has been so well received—not only in the English-speaking world, but, as its translation record shows, around the globe. The necessary task of updating and expanding the second edition in light of such serious global problems as the lingering global financial crisis, the Eurozone debt crisis, or the escalating climate crisis has made it difficult to keep a book on such a complex topic as 'globalization' short and accessible. This challenge becomes even more formidable in the case of a *very short* introduction. For this reason, the authors of the few existing short introductions to the subject have opted to concentrate on only one or two aspects of globalization—usually the digital revolution that created new information and communication technologies and the emerging global economic system, its history, structure, and supposed benefits and failings. While helpful in explaining the intricacies of international trade policy, global financial markets, worldwide flows of goods, services, and labour, transnational corporations, offshore financial centres, foreign direct investment, and the new international economic institutions, such narrow accounts often leave the general reader with a one-dimensional understanding of globalization as primarily an economic phenomenon mediated by cutting-edge information and communication technologies.

To be sure, the discussion of such economic and technological matters ought to be a significant part of any comprehensive account of globalization, but we should not stop there. The transformative powers of globalization reach deeply into *all* dimensions of contemporary social life. The present volume makes the case that globalization is best thought of as a multidimensional set of objective *and* subjective processes that resists confinement to any single thematic framework. In fact, globalization contains important *cultural* and *ideological* aspects in the form of politically charged meanings, stories, and symbols that define, describe, and analyse that very process. The social forces behind these competing accounts of globalization seek to endow this concept with norms, values, and understandings that not only legitimate and advance specific power interests, but also shape the personal and collective identities of billions of people. After all, it is mostly the question of whether globalization ought to be considered a 'good' or a 'bad' thing that has spawned heated debates in classrooms, boardrooms, and on the streets.

Moreover, the study of globalization extends beyond any single academic discipline. Yet, the lack of a firm disciplinary home also contains great opportunities. Global Studies has emerged as a new field of academic study that cuts across traditional disciplinary boundaries in the social sciences and humanities. This strong emphasis on transdisciplinarity requires students of global studies to familiarize themselves with vast literatures on related subjects that are usually studied in isolation from each other. The greatest challenge facing global studies lies, therefore, in connecting and synthesizing the various strands of knowledge in a way that does justice to the increasingly fluid and interdependent nature of our fast-changing, postmodern world. In short, Global Studies requires an approach broad enough to behold the 'big picture'. Such a transdisciplinary endeavour may well lead to the rehabilitation of the academic generalist whose prestige, for too long, has been overshadowed by the specialist.

Finally, let me add a word of clarification. Although the main purpose of this book is to provide its audience with a descriptive and explanatory account of the various dimensions of globalization, the careful reader will detect throughout a critical approach to certain forms of globalization. This pertains especially to the nature and the effects of what I call 'market globalism'. But my scepticism should not be interpreted as a blanket rejection of either markets or globalization. In fact, I appreciate the role of markets in facilitating necessary material exchanges. I also believe that we should take comfort in the fact that the world is becoming a more interdependent place that enhances people's chances to acknowledge their common humanity across arbitrarily drawn political borders and cultural divides. I also welcome the global flow of ideas and goods, as well as the sustainable development of technology, provided that they go hand in hand with greater forms of freedom and equality for *all* people, especially those living in the disadvantaged areas of the global South.

Humane forms of globalization are more attuned to what are shaping up to be two most daunting tasks facing us in the 21st century: the reduction of global disparities in wealth and wellbeing and the preservation of our wondrous planet. Thus, the brunt of my critique is not directed at globalization per se, but at particular manifestations and tendencies that strike me as falling short of the noble vision of a more equitable and sustainable global order.

It is a pleasant duty to record my debts of gratitude. I want to thank my colleagues and friends at the University of Hawai'i-Manoa and the Royal Melbourne Institute of Technology (RMIT University). Special thanks are due to Paul James, the Director of RMIT's Global Cities Research Institute, for his steady intellectual encouragement and loyal friendship. I appreciate the engagement of my colleagues from around the world who have channelled much of their enthusiasm for the study of globalization into the development of the Global Studies Consortium, a transcontinental professional organization dedicated to strengthening the new transdisciplinary field of Global Studies. I also want to express my deep appreciation to numerous readers, reviewers, and audiences around the world, who, for nearly two decades, have made insightful comments in response to my public lectures and publications on the subject of globalization. Dr. Franz Broswimmer, a dear friend and innovative social thinker, deserves special recognition for supplying me with valuable information on the ecological aspects of globalization. I want to thank Tim Strom, my Research Assistant at RMIT University, for helping me to locate relevant materials for this third edition. Andrea Keegan and Emma Marchant, my editors at Oxford University Press, have been shining examples of professionalism and competence. Finally, I want to thank my wife Perle—as well as the Steger and Besserman families—for their love and support. Many people have contributed to improving the quality of this book; its remaining flaws are my own responsibility.

List of abbreviations

AOL	America Online
APEC	Asian Pacific Economic Cooperation
ASEAN	Association of South East Asian Nations
BCE	Before the Common Era
CE	Common Era
CEO	Chief executive officer
CFCs	Chlorofluorocarbons
CITES	Convention on International Trade in Endangered Species of Wild Flora and Fauna
CNBC	Cable National Broadcasting Corporation
CNN	Cable News Network
EU	European Union
FIFA	*Fédération Internationale de Football Association* (International Federation of Football Associations)
FTAA	Free Trade Area of the Americas
G8	Group of Eight
G20	Group of Twenty
GATT	General Agreement of Tariffs and Trade
GCC	Global Climate Crisis
GDP	Gross domestic product
GFC	Global Financial Crisis
GNP	Gross national product
HIPC	Heavily Indebted Poor Countries Initiative
ICT	Information and Communication Technology
IMF	International Monetary Fund
INGO	International non-governmental organization
MAI	Multilateral Agreement on Investment
MERCOSUR	*Mercado Comun del Sur* (Southern Common Market)

MTV	Music Television
NAFTA	North American Free Trade Agreement
NATO	North Atlantic Treaty Organization
NGO	Non-governmental organization
OECD	Organization for Economic Co-operation and Development
OPEC	Organization of Petroleum Exporting Countries
TNCs	Transnational corporations
UN	United Nations
UNCTAD	United Nations Conference on Trade and Development
UNESCO	United Nations Educational, Scientific and Cultural Organization
WEF	World Economic Forum
WSF	World Social Forum
WTO	World Trade Organization

List of illustrations

1 Shakira performing *Waka Waka* at the 2010 FIFA World Cup Kick-off Concert, 10 June 2010 **8**
© Jon Hrusa/epa/Corbis

2 The globalization scholars and the elephant **12**
© Kenneth Panfilio and Ryan Canney

3 Assyrian clay tablet with cuneiform writing, *c.*1900–1800 BCE **23**
© Christie's Images/Corbis

4 The Great Wall of China **25**
© Corbis

5 The sale of the island of Manhattan in 1626 **30**
© Corbis/Bettmann

6 Bretton Woods Conference of 1944 **38**
© UN photo

7 The New York Stock Exchange **47**
© Gail Mooney/Corbis

8 The Security Council of the United Nations in session **64**
© Eskinder Debebe/UN Photo

9 Jihad vs McWorld: selling fast food in Indonesia **81**
© AP/Press Association Images

10 The greenhouse effect **93**
© Union of Concerned Scientists, USA

11 Microsoft CEO, Bill Gates **107**
© Ethan Miller/Corbis

12 WTO protestors in downtown Seattle, 30 November 1999 **123**
© Nick Cobbing/Rex Features

13 The burning twin towers of the World Trade Center, 11 September 2001 **126**
Sean Adair/STR, © Reuters 2001

14 Hundreds of thousands of protestors at Cairo's Tahrir Square, 20 April 2012 **133**
© Peer Grimm/dpa/Corbis

15 US President Barack Obama with German Chancellor Angela Merkel and Australian Prime Minister Julia Gillard at the G20 Summit in Los Cabos, Mexico, 19 June 2012 **134**
© Mosa'ab Elshamy/Demotix/Corbis

List of maps

1. Early human migrations 21
2. Major world trade networks, 1000–1450 27
3. Countries falling into recession as a result of the Global Financial Crisis, 2008 52
4. The European Union 71
5. Geography of the rich: number of people in thousands with investable assets of $1 million or more, 2010 114

List of figures

A. Global tourists to South Africa in June 2010 **3**
B. The global South: a fate worse than debt **44**
C. The advance of deregulation and liberalization, 1980–98 **46**
D. Transnational corporations versus countries: a comparison **55**
E. The nation-state in a globalizing world **69**
F. Incipient global governance: a network of interrelated power centres **72**
G. The American way of life **78**
H. The declining number of languages around the world, 1500–2000 **85**
I. Annual consumption patterns (per capita) in selected countries, 2010–12 **90**
J. Major manifestations and consequences of global environmental degradation **95**
K. The top 20 carbon dioxide emitters, 2008–10 **98**
L. Long term global CO_2 emissions **99**
M. Major global environmental treaties/conferences, 1971–2012 **101**
N. Income divergence in the USA, 1980–2010 **113**
O. Global Internet users as a percentage of the regional population **116**
P. Examples of justice-globalist organizations **119**

Chapter 1
Globalization: a contested concept

Although the earliest appearance of the term 'globalization' in the English language can be traced back to the 1940s, it was not until half a century later that this concept took the public consciousness by storm. The buzzword 'globalization' exploded into the 'Roaring Nineties' because it captured the increasingly interdependent nature of social life on our planet. Twenty years later, one can track millions of references to globalization in both virtual and printed space.

Unfortunately, however, early bestsellers on the subject—for example, Kenichi Ohmae's *The End of the Nation State* or Thomas Friedman's *The Lexus and the Olive Tree*—left their readers with the simplistic impression that globalization was an inevitable techno-economic juggernaut spreading the logic of capitalism and Western values by eradicating local traditions and national cultures. This influential notion of globalization as a steamroller flattening local, national, and regional scales also appeared as the spectre of 'Americanization' haunting the rest of the world. Such widespread fears or hopes—depending on how one felt about such forces of Westernization—deepened further in the 2000s during the so-called 'Global War on Terror' spearheaded by an 'American Empire' of worldwide reach. Even the more recent public debates about the alleged decline of the United States in the age of Obama and the corresponding rise of China and India have done little to soften this rigid dichotomy positing the West against the 'rest'. As a result, many people still have trouble recognizing globalization for what it is: the myriad forms of connectivity and flows linking the local (and national) to the global—as well as the West to the East, and the North to the South.

As an illustration of such a more nuanced understanding of globalization as a thickening 'global-local nexus'—or what some global studies scholars refer to as 'glocalization'—let us consider the world's most popular sports event: the Football World Cup. First organized in 1930 by the International Federation of Football Associations (FIFA), the event was soon seen as the ultimate national contest pitting country against country in the relentless pursuit of patriotic glory. The World Cup has since been held every four years (except for 1942 and 1946) in host countries located on all continents except Oceania. In fact, this transnational rotation of host countries coupled with the event's name 'World Cup' (instead of 'Nations Cup')—gives us a first indication of why the global should not be rigidly separated from the national. But let us delve more deeply into the matter and consider even more telling facts related to the 2010 World Cup to shed light on the complex 'glocal' dynamics that define the phenomenon we have come to call 'globalization'.

The global-local nexus and the South African World Cup

The nineteenth FIFA World Cup for men's national football was held from 11 June to 11 July 2010 in South Africa (see Figure A). The 32 best national teams from a total of 205 original contestants competed for the coveted golden globe trophy. These included six nations from Africa, three from Asia, thirteen from Europe, three from North Africa, six from South America, and two from Oceania. Played in ten stadiums located in nine South

African cities, the games drew hundreds of thousands of football tourists from around the world.

The global-local dynamics are rather obvious here: national teams playing in South African stadiums in front of a mixture of local and global spectators as well as virtual global audiences watching the games on TVs and other digital devices. Indeed, the 2010 FIFA World Cup was shown in every single country and territory on Earth. The in-home coverage of the competition reached over 3.2 billion people—47 per cent of the global population—who watched at least a few minutes of the event. A whopping 620 million people followed at least twenty consecutive minutes of the

Region/Country	**Number of tourists entering South Africa**	**% increase from June 2009**
Europe	124,752	**72**
England	40,903	**15**
France	11,451	**847**
Central & South America	47,188	**925**
Mexico	12,009	**5,334**
Brazil	14,100	**397**
North America	50,902	**100**
USA	44,894	**99**
Asia	30,914	**120**
India	6,561	**50**
Japan	5,793	**276**
Australasia	18,450	**136**
Australia	16,106	**155**
Middle East	5,139	**122**
Israel	2,747	**825**
Africa	398,085	**12**
Swaziland	45,591	**0.4**
Algeria	2,342	**1744**
World	721,311	**43**

A. Global tourists to South Africa in June 2010

Source: Statistics South Africa, June 2010, <www.statssa.gov.za/publications/P0351/P0351June2010.pdf>

championship match between victorious Spain and the Netherlands.

Related money matters are equally global-local in nature. The World Cup cost South Africa US$3.5 billion, including $1.2 billion for infrastructure upgrades, $1.2 billion for transport, and $387 million for broadcasting. However, $1.6 billion was raised in sponsorship revenue, with the most significant contracts signing such powerful transnational corporations (TNCs) as Adidas, Coca Cola, Visa, McDonalds, and BP. In the end, FIFA happily pocketed a handsome profit of $1 billion, which pushed the organization's 2010 revenue to above $4 billion.

The official World Cup match-ball, too, represents an impressive example of the glocal dynamics constituting globalization. Supplied by Adidas, a gigantic TNC headquartered in Germany, the football was given the name 'Jabulani' which means 'celebrate' in the Zulu language. In spite of their apparent local identity, however, all Jabulani balls were manufactured in China using a latex bladder made in India and a thermoplastic rubber produced in Taiwan. These plastics, in turn, were generated from petroleum imported from the Middle East and Norway, and carried on mostly South Korean built ships.

What do Diego Forlán and Shakira have in common?

But perhaps the most striking illustration of how globalization erupts simultaneously across all geographical scales involves two of the most celebrated superstars of the World Cup: Uruguayan striker Diego Forlán, the tournament's most valuable player, and Colombian singer-entertainer Shakira, who performed the official anthem of the 2010 World Cup at the opening and closing ceremonies of the mega-event.

Born in 1979 into a prominent football-playing family in Montevideo, Uruguay, Diego Forlán was sent from an early age to English-speaking schools. When his older sister Alejandra was left paralysed after a car accident, 12-year-old Diego resolved to earn enough money from a professional football career to pay her hospital bills and afford the best doctors. He kept his promise when, years later, he set up the Alejandra Forlán Foundation. He would also use his global celebrity status in public TV campaigns denouncing dangerous driving.

Launching his career with two Uruguayan football clubs, Forlán was transferred in 1998 to the top Argentinean club Atlético Independiente. Scoring thirty-six goals in only seventy-seven games, his global profile rose quickly. In 2002, he signed a contract with the famous English club Manchester United for a transfer sum of US$10.65 million. After three years, Forlán left England and joined, in short succession, the Spanish clubs Villareal and Atlético Madrid. Following the 2010 World Cup, he moved to Italy to play for Internazionale Milan, one of Europe's premier football clubs. In June 2012, Diego's abiding global popularity was reflected in the staggering 2,732,586 'likes' gracing his Facebook page.

But Diego Forlán's greatest moments came in South Africa where he led his national team to an impressive fourth place finish. This made Uruguay the most successful South American country of the World Cup, surpassing football giants Brazil and Argentina. Proudly wearing the blue and black colours of his nation, Forlán dazzled local and global fans with his speed, elegance, and goal scoring instincts. Not only did he finish as the tournament's joint top scorer, but he also won the Golden Ball for the best player of the World Cup.

Diego Forlán and many of his fellow footballers performing in South African stadiums thus embodied the 'glocal' dynamics of globalization as they played for national teams that entertained local and global audiences while at the same time a large part of their football identity remained firmly linked to their contracted clubs in global cities around the world.

A careful deconstruction of World Cup entertainer Shakira reveals even more clearly why we should not approach globalization as a disconnected phenomenon floating above the local and national. Shakira Isabel Mebarak Ripoll was born on 2 February 1977 in Barranquilla, Colombia, to a New York City-born father of Arabic background and a mother of Spanish-Catalan descent. A native Spanish speaker, Shakira showed particular talent for languages and was soon fluent in English and Portuguese, in addition to acquiring some Italian, French, Catalan, and Arabic. She began performing as a singer and dancer at a young age and broke through in 1998 as a rock and roll artist with strong Latin and Arabic influences, when her album *Dónde Están los Ladrones?* sold over seven million copies worldwide. In many ways, both Shakira's personal background and her style of music can be characterized in terms of 'hybridization'—the mixing of different cultural elements and styles. As we will explore in more detail in Chapter 5 of this book, these cultural hybridization processes have been greatly accelerated by globalization.

By 2010, Shakira had become one of the top female superstars in the global entertainment business, having won two Grammy Awards, eight Latin Grammy Awards, twelve Billboard Latin Music Awards, and one Golden Globe nomination. On 10 June of that year, the golden-maned, barefoot superstar took centre stage at FIFA's first-ever Kick-off Concert in Johannesburg's Orlando Stadium, accompanied by the popular South African band *Freshly Ground*. To the delight of tens of thousands of local revellers and millions of digital viewers around the world, Shakira wore what was described as 'African regalia' by its designer, Italian fashion Czar Roberto Cavalli. The global-local ensemble consisted of a silk-fringed, grass-like skirt loosely worn over a zebra-print jumpsuit drastically reduced in size by deep side cut-outs. 'African accessories' such as massive leather fringe bracelets and huge silver disc earrings completed Shakira's fantasy costume (see Illustration 1).

Similar hybrid, global-local creations of material culture are also reflected in the 2010 World Cup anthem *Waka Waka*—controversially translated into English as 'This Time for Africa'. The words and music in the version performed by Shakira stem from the traditional Cameroonian war song 'Zangawela'. First recorded in the 1980s by the African group *Golden Sounds*, the song was picked up a few years later by the Latin American songwriter Wilfrido Vargas. His faster version of *Waka Waka* in turn inspired numerous versions in France, Holland, Suriname, Senegal, Jamaica, and other countries. Shakira's World Cup rendition of *Waka Waka* quickly turned into a global earworm, selling more than four million copies worldwide. Her video clip on YouTube has become the third most watched music video of all time with over 250 million views. And yet, *Golden Sounds* benefitted little from the global success of the song since the band did not have the resources to sue SONY, Shakira's powerful recording label. Ultimately, however, the transnational media giant settled with the Cameroonian musicians to avoid bad publicity over growing charges of possible copyright piracy.

So what—in addition to their multilingual upbringing and their remarkable talent—do the Colombian pop star performing a remixed version of an already globalized World Cup anthem and a Uruguayan football striker playing for various European city clubs have in common? They are both the products and catalysts of globalization processes that make more sense when considered as a global-local nexus. In short, globalization cannot be confined to macro-dynamics isolated from concrete settings but as complex connections and flows linking the global to the local and vice versa. Our deconstruction of the 2010 World Cup has prepared us to tackle the rather demanding task of assembling a working definition of a contested concept that has proven notoriously hard to pin down.

1. Shakira performing *Waka Waka* at the 2010 FIFA World Cup Kick-off Concert, 10 June 2010

Towards a definition of globalization

'Globalization' has been variously used in both the popular press and academic literature to describe a process, a condition, a system, a force, and an age. Given that these competing labels have very different meanings, their indiscriminate usage is often obscure and invites confusion. For example, a sloppy conflation of process and condition encourages circular definitions that explain little. The often repeated truism that globalization (the process) leads to more globalization (the condition) does not allow us to draw meaningful analytical distinctions between causes and effects.

Hence, I suggest that we adopt the term *globality* to signify a *social condition* characterized by tight global economic, political, cultural, and environmental interconnections and flows that make most of the currently existing borders and boundaries irrelevant. Yet, we should not assume either that globality is already upon us nor that it refers to a determinate endpoint that precludes any further development. Rather, this concept signifies a future social condition that, like all conditions, is destined to give way to new constellations. For example, it is conceivable that globality might eventually be transformed into something we might call 'planetarity'—a new social condition brought about by the successful colonization of our solar system. Moreover, we could easily imagine different social manifestations of globality: one might be based primarily on values of individualism, competition, and laissez-faire capitalism, while another might draw on more communal and cooperative norms. These possible alternatives point to the fundamentally *indeterminate character* of globality.

The term *globalization* applies to a *set of social processes* that appear to transform our present social condition of conventional nationality into one of globality. As we noted in our observations about the 2010 World Cup, however, this does not mean that the national or the local are becoming extinct or irrelevant. In fact, the national and local are changing their character as a result of our movement towards globality. At its core, then, globalization is about shifting forms of human contact. Indeed, any affirmation of globalization implies three assertions: first, that we are slowly leaving behind the condition of modern nationality that gradually unfolded from the 18th century onwards; second, that we are moving towards the new condition of postmodern globality; and, third, that we have not yet reached it. Indeed, like 'modernization' and other verbal nouns that end in the suffix '-ization', the term 'globalization' suggests a sort of dynamism best captured by the notion of 'development' or 'unfolding' along discernible patterns. Such unfolding may occur quickly or slowly, but it always corresponds to the idea of change, and, therefore, denotes transformation.

Hence, academics exploring the dynamics of globalization are particularly keen on pursuing research questions related to the theme of social change. How does globalization proceed? What is driving it? Does it have one cause or is there a combination of factors? Is globalization a continuation of modernity or is it a radical break? Does it create new forms of inequality and hierarchy? Notice that the conceptualization of globalization as a dynamic process rather than as a static condition forces the researcher to pay close attention to our shifting perceptions of time and space mediated by digital technology.

Finally, let us adopt *global imaginary* as a concept referring to people's growing consciousness of global connectivity. Again, as we have seen in our deconstruction of the 2010 World Cup, this is not to say that national and local communal frameworks have lost their power to provide people with a meaningful sense of home and identity. But it would be a mistake to close one's eyes to the weakening of the national imaginary as it has been historically constituted in the 19th and 20th centuries. The thickening of the global consciousness destabilizes and unsettles the conventional nation-state within which people imagine their communal existence. As we shall see in Chapter 7, the rising global imaginary is also powerfully reflected in the current transformation of the principal ideas and values that go into the articulation of concrete political agendas and programs.

To argue that globalization constitutes a set of social processes enveloped by the rising global imaginary that propel us towards the condition of globality may eliminate the danger of circular definitions, but it gives us only one defining characteristic of the process: movement towards more intense forms of connectivity and integration. But such a general definition of globalization tells us little about its remaining qualities. In order to overcome this deficiency, it behoves us to identify additional qualities that make globalization different from other sets of social processes. Yet, whenever researchers raise the level of specificity in order to bring the phenomenon in question into sharper focus, they also heighten the danger of provoking scholarly disagreements over definitions. Our subject is no exception. One of the reasons why globalization remains a contested concept is because there exists no scholarly consensus on what kinds of social processes constitute its essence.

After all, globalization is an uneven process, meaning that people living in various parts of the world are affected very differently by this gigantic transformation of social structures and cultural zones. Hence, the social processes that make up globalization have been analysed and explained by various commentators in different, often contradictory ways. Scholars not only hold different views with regard to proper definitions of globalization, they also disagree on its scale, causation, chronology, impact, trajectories, and policy outcomes. The ancient Buddhist parable of the blind scholars and their encounter with the elephant helps to illustrate the academic controversy over the nature and various dimensions of globalization.

Since the blind scholars did not know what the elephant looked like, they resolved to obtain a mental picture, and thus the knowledge they desired, by touching the animal. Feeling its trunk, one blind man argued that the elephant was like a lively snake. Another man, rubbing along its enormous leg, likened the animal to a rough column of massive proportions. The third person took hold of its tail and insisted that the elephant resembled a large, flexible brush. The fourth man felt its sharp tusks and declared it to be like a great spear. Each of the blind scholars held firmly to his own idea of what constituted an elephant. Since their scholarly reputation was riding on the veracity of their respective findings, the blind men eventually ended up arguing over the true nature of the elephant. (See Illustration 2).

The ongoing academic quarrel over which dimension contains the essence of globalization represents a postmodern version of the parable of the blind men and the elephant. Even those few remaining scholars who still think of globalization as a singular process clash with each other over which aspect of social life constitutes its primary domain. Many global studies experts argue that economic processes lie at the core of globalization. Others privilege political, cultural, or ideological aspects. Still others

2. The globalization scholars and the elephant

point to environmental processes as being the essence of globalization. Like the blind men in the parable, each globalization researcher is partly right by correctly identifying *one* important dimension of the phenomenon in question. However, their collective mistake lies in their dogmatic attempts to reduce such a complex phenomenon as globalization to one or two domains that corresponds to their own expertise. Surely, a central task for the new field of global studies must be to devise better ways for gauging the relative importance of each dimension without losing sight of the interdependent whole.

Despite such differences of opinion, it is nonetheless possible to detect some thematic overlap in various scholarly attempts to identify the core qualities of globalization processes. Consider, for example, the following influential definitions of globalization:

Globalization can thus be defined as the intensification of worldwide social relations which link distant localities in such a way that local happenings are shaped by events occurring many miles away and vice versa. (Anthony Giddens, Former Director of the London School of Economics)

Globalization may be thought of as a process (or set of processes) which embodies a transformation in the spatial organization of social relations and transactions—assessed in terms of their extensity, intensity, velocity and impact—generating transcontinental or interregional flows and networks of activity, interaction, and the exercise of power. (David Held, Professor of Politics and International Relations, Durham University)

Globalization as a concept refers both to the compression of the world and the intensification of consciousness of the world as a whole. (Roland Robertson, Emeritus Professor of Sociology, University of Aberdeen, Scotland)

These definitions point to four additional qualities or characteristics at the core of globalization. First, it involves both the *creation* of new social networks and the *multiplication* of existing connections that cut across traditional political, economic, cultural, and geographical boundaries. As we have seen in the case of the 2010 World Cup, today's media combine conventional TV coverage with multiple feeds into digital devices and networks that transcend nationally based services.

The second quality of globalization is reflected in the *expansion* and the *stretching* of social relations, activities, and connections. Today's financial markets reach around the globe, and electronic trading occurs around the clock. Gigantic and virtually identical shopping malls have emerged on all continents, catering to those consumers who can afford commodities from all regions of the world—including products whose various components were manufactured in different countries. This process of social stretching applies to FIFA as well as to other non-governmental organizations, commercial enterprises, social clubs, and countless regional and global institutions and associations: the UN, the EU, the Association of South East Asian Nations, the Organization of African Unity, Doctors Without Borders, the World Social Forum, and Google, to name but a few.

Third, globalization involves the *intensification* and *acceleration* of social exchanges and activities. As the Spanish sociologist Manuel Castells has pointed out, the creation of a global network society fuelled by 'communication power' required a technological revolution—one that has been powered chiefly by the rapid development of new information and communication technologies. Proceeding at breakneck speed, these innovations are reshaping the social landscape of human life. The World Wide Web relays distant information in real time, and satellites provide consumers with instant pictures of remote events. Sophisticated social networking by means of Facebook or Twitter has become a routine activity for more than a billion people around the globe.

The intensification of worldwide social relations means that local happenings are shaped by events occurring far away, and vice versa. To make the point again, the seemingly opposing processes of globalization and localization actually imply each other. Rather than sitting at the base and the top of conventional geographical hierarchies, the local and global intermingle, sometimes messily, with the national and regional, in overlapping horizontal scales.

Fourth, as we emphasized in our definition of the global imaginary, globalization processes do not occur merely on an objective, material level but they also involve the subjective plane of human consciousness. Without erasing local and national attachments, the compression of the world into a single place has increasingly made global the frame of reference for human thought and action. Hence, globalization involves both the macro-structures of a 'global community' and the micro-structures of 'global personhood'. It extends deep into the core of the self and its dispositions, facilitating the creation of multiple individual and collective identities nurtured by the intensifying relations between the personal and the global.

Having succinctly identified some of the core qualities of globalization, let us compress them into a single sentence that yields the following *very short* definition of globalization:

> Globalization refers to the expansion and intensification of social relations and consciousness across world-time and world-space.

Before we draw this chapter to a close, we should consider an important objection raised by global studies scholars sensitive to historical matters: Is globalization really all that different from the centuries-old process of modernization? Some critics have responded to this question in the negative, contending that even a cursory look at history suggests that there is not much that is new about contemporary globalization. Hence, before we explore in some detail the main dimensions of globalization in subsequent chapters of this book, we should give this argument a fair hearing. After all, such a critical investigation of globalization's alleged novelty and its relationship to modernity are closely related to yet another question hotly debated in global studies: What does a proper chronology and historical periodization of globalization look like? Let us turn to Chapter 2 to find answers to these questions.

Chapter 2
Globalization and history: is globalization a new phenomenon?

If we asked an ordinary person on the busy streets of global cities like New York, Shanghai, or Sydney about the essence of globalization, the answer would probably involve some reference to growing forms of connectivity fuelled by exploding information and communication technologies. People might point to their ultra-thin laptop computers; all sorts of mobile devices such as Cloud-connected smart wireless phones and tablets like the popular iPhone or the Kindle Fire; powerful Internet search engines like Google that sort in a split-second through gigantic data sets; individual video-postings on YouTube; ubiquitous social networking sites like Twitter; the rapidly expanding blogosphere, satellite- and computer-connected HDTVs; interactive 3-D computer and video games; the new generation of super-jetliners like the Airbus A380 or Boeing's Dreamliner; and the international space station.

As important as technology is for the intensification of global connectivity, it provides only a partial explanation for the latest wave of globalization since the 1980s. Yet, it would be foolish to deny that these new innovations have played a crucial role in the compression of world-time and world-space. The Internet, in particular, has assumed a pivotal function in facilitating globalization through the creation of the World Wide Web that connects billions of individuals, civil society associations, and governments. Since most of these technologies have been around for less than three decades, it seems to make sense to agree with those commentators who claim that globalization is, indeed, a relatively new phenomenon.

Still, the definition of globalization we arrived at in the previous chapter stresses the dynamic nature of the phenomenon. The global expansion of social relations and the rise of the global imaginary are gradual processes with deep historical roots. The engineers who developed personal computers and supersonic jet planes stand on the shoulders of earlier innovators who created the steam engine, the cotton gin, the telegraph, the phonograph, the telephone, the typewriter, the internal-combustion engine, and electrical appliances. These products, in turn, owe their existence to much earlier technological inventions such as the telescope, the compass, water wheels, windmills, gunpowder, the printing press, and oceangoing ships. In order to acknowledge the full historical record, we might reach back even further to such momentous technological and social achievements as the production of paper, the development of writing, the invention of the wheel, the domestication of wild plants and animals, the slow outward migration of our common African ancestors, and, finally, the emergence of language at the dawn of human evolution.

Thus, the answer to the question of whether globalization constitutes a new phenomenon depends upon how far we are willing to extend the web of causation that resulted in those recent technologies and social arrangements that most people have come to associate with our buzzword. Some scholars consciously limit the historical scope of globalization to the post-1989 era in order to capture its contemporary uniqueness. Others are willing to extend this timeframe to include the ground-breaking developments of the last two centuries. Still others argue that globalization really represents the continuation and extension of complex processes that began with the emergence of modernity and the capitalist world system in the 1500s. And a few remaining researchers refuse to confine globalization to time periods measured in mere decades or centuries. Rather, they suggest that these processes have been unfolding for millennia.

No doubt, each of these contending perspectives contains important insights. As we will see in subsequent chapters, the advocates of the first approach have marshalled impressive evidence for their view that the dramatic expansion and acceleration of global exchanges since the 1980s represents a quantum leap in the history of globalization. The proponents of the second view correctly emphasize the tight connection between contemporary forms of globalization and the explosion of technology known as the Industrial Revolution. The representatives of the third perspective rightly point to the significance of the time-space compression that occurred in the 16th century when Eurasia, Africa, and the Americas first became connected by enduring trade routes. Finally, the advocates of the fourth approach advance a rather sensible argument when they insist that any truly comprehensive account of globalization falls short without the incorporation of ancient developments and enduring dynamics into our planetary history.

While the short chronology outlined below is necessarily fragmentary and general, it identifies five historical periods that are separated from each other by significant accelerations in the pace of social exchanges as well as a widening of their geographical scope. Thus, we could say that globalization is an ancient process that, over many centuries, has crossed distinct qualitative thresholds. In this context, it is important to bear in mind that my chronology does not necessarily imply a linear unfolding of history, nor does it advocate a conventional Eurocentric perspective of world history. Full of unanticipated surprises, violent twists, sudden punctuations, and dramatic reversals, the history of globalization has involved all major regions and cultures of our planet.

The prehistoric period (10,000 BCE–3500 BCE)

Let us begin 12,000 years ago when small bands of hunters and gatherers reached the southern tip of South America. This event marked the end of the long process of settling all five continents that was begun by our hominid African ancestors more than one million years ago. Although some major island groups in the Pacific and the Atlantic were not inhabited until relatively recent times, the truly global dispersion of our species was finally achieved. The successful endeavour of the South American nomads rested on the migratory achievements of their Siberian ancestors who had crossed the Bering Strait into North America at least a thousand years earlier.

In this earliest phase of globalization, contact among thousands of hunter and gatherer bands spread all over the world was geographically limited and mostly coincidental. This fleeting mode of social interaction changed dramatically about 10,000 years ago when humans took the crucial step of producing their own food. As a result of several factors, including the natural occurrence of plants and animals suitable for domestication as well as continental differences in area and total population size, only certain regions located on or near the vast Eurasian landmass proved to be ideal for these growing agricultural settlements. These areas were located in the Fertile Crescent, north-central China, North Africa, northwestern India, and New Guinea. Over time, food surpluses achieved by these early farmers and herders led to population increases, the establishment of permanent villages, and the construction of fortified towns.

Roving bands of nomads lost out to settled tribes, chiefdoms, and, ultimately, powerful states based on agricultural food production. (See Map 1). The decentralized, egalitarian nature of hunter and gatherer groups was replaced by centralized and highly stratified patriarchal social structures headed by chiefs and priests who were exempted from hard manual labour. Moreover, for the first

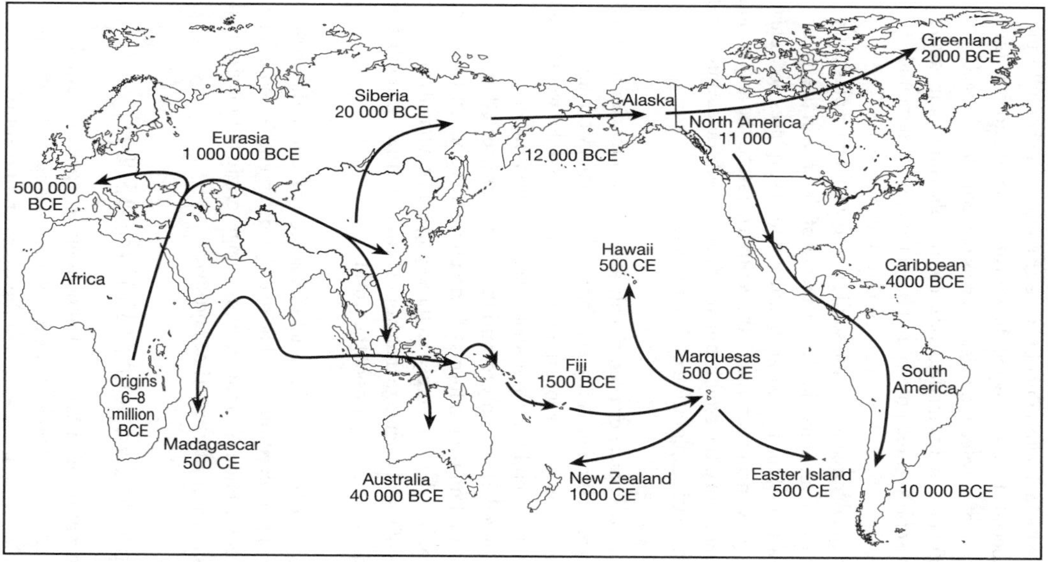
Greenland
2000 BCE
Alaska
North America
11 000
Siberia
20 000 BCE
Eurasia
1 000 000 BCE
12.000 BCE
500 000
BCE
Africa
Hawaii
500 CE
Caribbean
4000 BCE
Marquesas
500 OCE
Fiji
1500 BCE
South
America
Origins
6–8
million
BCE
Madagascar
500 CE
Australia
40 000 BCE
New Zealand
1000 CE
Easter Island
500 CE
10 000 BCE

Map 1. Early human migrations

time in human history, these farming societies were able to support two additional social classes whose members did not participate in food production. One group consisted of full-time craft specialists who directed their creative energies toward the invention of new technologies, such as powerful iron tools, beautiful ornaments made of precious metals, complex irrigation canals, sophisticated pottery and basketry, and monumental building structures. The other group was comprised of professional bureaucrats and soldiers who would later play a key role in the monopolization of the means of violence in the hands of a few rulers, the precise accounting of food surpluses necessary for the growth and survival of the centralized state, the acquisition of new territory, the establishment of permanent trade routes, and the systematic exploration of distant regions.

For the most part, however, globalization in the prehistoric period was severely limited. Advanced forms of technology capable of overcoming existing geographical and social obstacles were largely absent; thus, enduring long-distance interactions never materialized. It was only toward the end of this epoch that centrally administered forms of agriculture, religion, bureaucracy, and warfare slowly emerged as the key agents of intensifying modes of social exchange that would involve a growing number of societies in many regions of the world.

Perhaps the best way of characterizing the dynamic of this earliest phase of globalization would be to call it 'divergence'—people and social connections stemming from a single origin but moving and diversifying greatly over time and space.

The premodern period (3500 BCE–1500 CE)

The invention of writing in Mesopotamia, Egypt, and central China between 3500 and 2000 BCE (see Illustration 3) roughly coincided with the invention of the wheel around 3000 BCE in Southwest Asia. Marking the close of the prehistoric period, these

3. Assyrian clay tablet with cuneiform writing, *c*.1900–1800 BCE

monumental inventions amounted to one of those technological and social boosts that moved globalization to a new level. Thanks to the auspicious east-west orientation of Eurasia's major continental axis—a geographical feature that had already facilitated the rapid spread of crops and animals suitable for food production along the same latitudes—the diffusion of these new technologies to distant parts of the continent occurred within only a few centuries. The importance of these inventions for the strengthening of globalization processes should be obvious. Among other things, the wheel spurred crucial infrastructural innovations such as animal-drawn carts and permanent roads that allowed for the faster and more efficient transportation of people and goods. In addition to the spread of ideas and inventions, writing greatly facilitated the coordination of complex social activities and thus encouraged large state formations. Of the sizeable territorial units that arose during this period, only the Andes civilizations of South America managed to grow into the mighty Inca Empire without the benefits of either the wheel or the written word.

The later premodern period was the age of empires. As some states succeeded in establishing permanent rule over other states, the resulting vast territorial accumulations formed the basis of the Egyptian Kingdoms, the Persian Empire, the Macedonian Empire, the American Empires of the Aztecs and the Incas, the Roman Empire, the Indian Empires, the Byzantine Empire, the Islamic Caliphates, the Holy Roman Empire, the African Empires of Ghana, Mali, and Songhay, and the Ottoman Empire. All of these empires fostered the multiplication and extension of long-distance communication and the exchange of culture, technology, commodities, and diseases. The most enduring and technologically advanced of these vast premodern conglomerates was undoubtedly the Chinese Empire. A closer look at its history reveals some of the early dynamics of globalization.

After centuries of warfare between several independent states, the Qin Emperor's armies, in 221 BCE, finally unified large portions of northeast China. For the next 1,700 years, successive dynasties known as the Han, Sui, T'ang, Yuan, and Ming ruled an empire supported by vast bureaucracies that would extend its influence to such distant regions as tropical Southeast Asia, the Mediterranean, India, and East Africa (see Illustration 4). Dazzling artistry and brilliant philosophical achievements stimulated new discoveries in other fields of knowledge such as astronomy, mathematics, and chemistry. The long list of major technological innovations achieved in China during the premodern period include redesigned plowshares, hydraulic engineering, gunpowder, the tapping of natural gas, the

4. The Great Wall of China, begun in the 7th century BCE by warlords, was enlarged and rebuilt repeatedly

compass, mechanical clocks, paper, printing, lavishly embroidered silk fabrics, and sophisticated metalworking techniques. The construction of vast irrigation systems consisting of hundreds of small canals enhanced the region's agricultural productivity while at the same time providing for one of the best river transport systems in the world. The codification of law and the fixing of weights, measures, and values of coinage fostered the expansion of trade and markets. The standardization of the size of cart axles and the roads they travelled on allowed Chinese merchants for the first time to make precise calculations as to the desired quantities of imported and exported goods.

The most extensive of these trade routes was the Silk Road. It linked the Chinese and the Roman Empires, with Parthian traders serving as skilled intermediaries. Even 1,300 years after the Silk Road first reached the Italian peninsula, in 50 BCE, a truly multicultural group of Eurasian and African globetrotters—including the famous Moroccan merchant Ibn Battuta and his Venetian counterparts in the Marco Polo family—relied on this great Eurasian land route to reach the splendid imperial court of the Mongol Khans in Beijing.

By the 15th century CE, enormous Chinese fleets consisting of hundreds of 400-foot-long ocean-going ships were crossing the Indian Ocean and establishing short-lived trade outposts on the east coast of Africa. However, a few decades later, the rulers of the Chinese Empire implemented a series of fateful political decisions that halted overseas navigation and mandated a retreat from further technological development. Thus, the rulers cut short their empire's incipient industrial revolution, a development that allowed much smaller European states to emerge as the primary historical agents behind the intensification of globalization.

Toward the end of the premodern period, then, the existing global trade network (see Map 2) consisted of several interlocking trade circuits that connected the most populous regions of Eurasia and northeastern Africa. Although both the Australian and the American continents still remained separate from this expanding web of economic, political, and cultural interdependence, the empires of the Aztecs and Incas had also succeeded in developing major trade networks in their own hemisphere.

The existence of these sprawling networks of economic and cultural exchange triggered massive waves of migration, which, in turn, led to further population increase and the rapid growth of urban centres. In the resulting cultural clashes, religions with only local significance were transformed into the major 'world religions' we know today as Judaism, Christianity, Islam, Hinduism, and Buddhism. But higher population density and more intense social interaction over greater distances also facilitated the spread of new infectious diseases like the bubonic plague. The enormous plague epidemic of the mid-14th century,

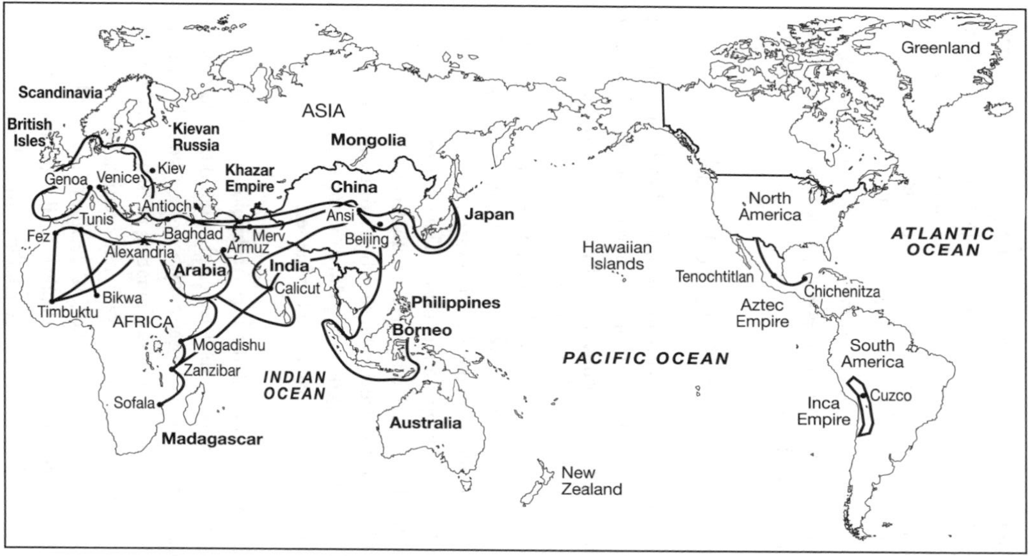

Map 2. Major world trade networks, 1000–1450

for example, killed up to one-third of the respective populations of China, the Middle East, and Europe. However, these unwelcome by-products of unfolding globalization processes did not reach their most horrific manifestation until the fateful 16th-century collision of the 'old' and 'new' worlds. Although the precise population size of the Americas before contact remains a contentious issue, it is estimated that the deadly germs of European invaders killed an estimated 18–20 million Native Americans—an inconceivable 90–95 per cent of the total indigenous population.

The early modern period (1500–1750)

The term 'modernity' has become associated with the 18th-century European Enlightenment project of developing objective science, achieving a universal form of morality and law, and liberating rational modes of thought and social organization from the perceived irrationalities of myth, religion, and political tyranny. But it is important to acknowledge the existence of multiple forms of modernity that often developed in various parts of the world in resistance to European modernity. The label 'early modern', then, refers to the period between the European Renaissance and the Enlightenment. During these two centuries, Europe and its social practices emerged as the primary catalyst for globalization after a long period of Asian predominance.

Indeed, having contributed little to technology and other civilizational achievements between about 500 CE–1000 CE, Europeans north of the Alps greatly benefited from the diffusion of technological innovations originating in Islamic and Chinese cultural spheres. Despite the weakened political influence of China and the noticeable ecological decline of the Fertile Crescent some 500 years later, European powers failed to penetrate into the interior of Africa and Asia. Instead, they turned their expansionistic desires westward, searching for a new, profitable sea route to India. Their efforts were aided by such innovations as mechanized printing, sophisticated wind and water mills, extensive postal systems, revised maritime technologies, and advanced navigation techniques. Add the enormous impact of the Reformation and the related liberal political idea of limited government, and we have identified the main forces behind the qualitative leap that greatly intensified demographic, cultural, ecological, and economic flows between Europe, Africa, and the Americas.

Of course, the rise of European metropolitan centres and their affiliated merchant classes represented another important factor responsible for strengthening globalization tendencies during the early modern period. Embodying the new values of individualism and unlimited material accumulation, European economic entrepreneurs laid the foundation of what later scholars would call the 'capitalist world system'. However, these fledgling capitalists could not have achieved the global expansion of their commercial enterprises without substantial support from their respective governments. The monarchs of Spain, Portugal, the Netherlands, France, and England all put significant resources into the exploration of new worlds and the construction of new interregional markets that benefited them much more than their exotic 'trading partners'.

By the early 1600s, national joint stock companies like the Dutch and British East India companies were founded for the express purpose of setting up profitable overseas trade posts. As these innovative corporations grew in size and stature, they acquired the power to regulate most intercontinental economic transactions, in the process implementing social institutions and cultural practices that enabled later colonial governments to place these foreign regions under direct political rule (see Illustration 5). Related developments, such as the Atlantic slave trade and forced population transfers within the Americas, resulted in the suffering and death of millions of non-Europeans while greatly benefiting white immigrants and their home countries.

5. The sale of the island of Manhattan in 1626

To be sure, religious warfare within Europe also created its share of dislocation and displacement for Caucasian populations. Moreover, as a result of these protracted armed conflicts, military alliances and political arrangements underwent continuous modification. This highlights the crucial role of warfare as a catalyst of globalization. Evolving from the Westphalian states system, the sovereign, territorial nation-state emerged in 18th-century Europe as the modern container of social life. As the early modern period drew to a close, interdependencies among nation-states were multiplying as well as increasing in density.

The modern period (1750–1980)

By the late 18th century, Australia and the Pacific islands were slowly incorporated into the European-dominated network of political, economic, and cultural exchange. Increasingly confronted with stories of the 'distant' and images of countless 'Others', Europeans and their descendants on other continents took it upon themselves to assume the role of the world's guardians of civilization and morality. In spite of their persistent claims to universal leadership, however, they remained strangely oblivious to their racist practices and the appalling conditions of inequality that existed both within their own societies and between the global North and South. Fed by a steady stream of materials and resources that originated mostly in other regions of the world, Western capitalist enterprises gained in stature. Daring to resist powerful governmental controls, economic entrepreneurs and their academic counterparts began to spread a philosophy of individualism and rational self-interest that glorified the virtues of an idealized capitalist system supposedly based upon the providential workings of the free market and its 'invisible hand'.

Written in 1847 by the German political radicals Karl Marx and Friedrich Engels, the passage below taken from their famous *Communist Manifesto* captures the qualitative shift in social relations that pushed globalization to a new level in the modern period.

Marx and Engels on globalization

The discovery of America prepared the way for mighty industry and its creation of a truly global market. The latter greatly expanded trade, navigation, and communication by land. These developments, in turn, caused the further expansion of industry. The growth of industry, trade, navigation, and railroads also went hand in hand with the rise of the bourgeoisie and capital which pushed to the background the old social classes of the Middle Ages... Chased around the globe by its burning desire for ever-expanding markets for its products, the bourgeoisie has no choice but settle everywhere; cultivate everywhere; establish connections everywhere... Rapidly improving the instruments of production, the bourgeoisie utilizes the incessantly easing modes of communication to pull all nations into civilization—even the most barbarian ones... In a nutshell, it creates the world in its own image. (Translated by the author)

Indeed, the volume of world trade increased dramatically between 1850 and 1914. Guided by the activities of multinational banks, capital and goods flowed across the borders relatively freely as the sterling-based gold standard made possible the worldwide circulation of leading national currencies like the British pound and the Dutch gilder. Eager to acquire their own independent resource bases, most European nation-states subjected large portions of the global South to direct colonial rule. On the eve of World War I, merchandise trade measured as a percentage of gross national output totalled almost 12 per cent for the industrialized countries, a level unmatched until the 1970s. Global pricing systems facilitated trade in important commodities like grains, cotton, and various metals. Brand name packaged goods like Coca-Cola drinks, Campbell soups, Singer sewing machines, and Remington typewriters made their first appearance. In order to raise the global visibility of these corporations, international advertising agencies launched the first full-blown trans-border commercial promotion campaigns.

As Marx and Engels noted, however, the rise of the European bourgeoisie and the related intensification of global interconnections would not have been possible without the 19th-century explosion of science and technology. To be sure, the maintenance of these new industrial regimes required new power sources such as electricity and petroleum. The largely unregulated use of these energy sources resulted in the annihilation of countless animal and plant species as well as the toxification of entire regions. On the up side, however, railways, mechanized shipping, and 20th-century intercontinental air transport managed to overcome the last remaining geographical obstacles to the establishment of a genuine global infrastructure, while at the same time lowering transportation costs.

These innovations in transportation were complemented by the swift development of communication technologies. The telegraph and its transatlantic reach after 1866 provided for instant information exchanges between the two hemispheres. Moreover, the telegraph set the stage for the telephone and wireless radio communication, prompting newly emerging communication corporations like AT&T to coin advertising slogans in celebration of a world 'inextricably bound together'. Finally, the 20th-century arrival of mass circulation newspapers and magazines, film, and television further enhanced a growing consciousness of a rapidly shrinking world.

The modern period also witnessed an unprecedented population explosion. Having increased only modestly from about 300 million at the time of the birth of Christ to 760 million in 1750, the world's population reached 3.7 billion in 1970. Enormous waves of migration intensified existing cultural exchanges and transformed traditional social patterns. Popular immigration countries like the United States of America, Canada, and Australia took advantage of this boost in productivity. By the early 20th century, these countries entered the world stage as forces to be reckoned with. At the same time, however, they made significant efforts to control these large migratory flows, in the process inventing novel forms of bureaucratic control and developing new surveillance techniques designed to accumulate more information about nationals while keeping 'undesirables' out.

When the accelerating process of industrialization sharpened existing disparities in wealth and wellbeing beyond bearable limits, many working people in the global North began to organize themselves politically in various labour movements and socialist parties. However, their idealistic calls for international class solidarity went largely unheeded. Instead, ideologies that translated the national imaginary into extreme political programs captured the imagination of millions of people around the world. There is no question that interstate rivalries intensified at the outset of the 20th century as a result of mass migration, urbanization, colonial competition, and the excessive liberalization of world trade. The ensuing period of extreme nationalism culminated in two devastating world wars, genocides, a long global economic depression, and hostile measures to protect narrowly conceived political communities.

The end of World War II saw the explosion of two powerful atomic bombs that killed 200,000 Japanese, most of them civilians. Nothing did more to convince people around the world of the linked fate of geographically and politically separated 'nations'. Indeed, the global imaginary found a horrifying expression in the Cold-War acronym 'MAD' (mutually assured destruction). A more positive result was the process of decolonization in the 1950s and 1960s that slowly revived global flows and international exchanges. A new political order of sovereign but interdependent nation-states anchored in the charter of the United Nations raised the prospect of global democratic governance. However, such cosmopolitan hopes quickly faded as the Cold War divided the world for four long decades into two antagonistic spheres: a liberal-capitalist 'First World' dominated by the United States, and an authoritarian-socialist 'Second World' controlled by the Soviet Union. Both blocs sought to establish their political and ideological dominance in the 'Third World'. Indeed, superpower confrontations like the Cuban Missile Crisis raised the spectre of a global conflict capable of destroying virtually all life on our planet.

The contemporary period (from the 1980s)

As we noted at the beginning of this chapter, the dramatic creation, expansion, and acceleration of worldwide interdependencies and global exchanges that have occurred since the early 1980s represent yet another quantum leap in the history of globalization. The best way of characterizing this latest globalization wave would be to call it 'convergence'—different and widely spaced people and social connections coming together more rapidly than ever before. This dynamic received another boost with the 1991 collapse of the communist Soviet Empire and 'neoliberal' attempts to create a single global market. Indeed, the deregulation of national economies combined with the Information and Communication Technology (ICT) Revolution kicked globalization into a new gear. The unprecedented development of horizontal networks of interactive communication that connected the local and global was made possible through the worldwide diffusion of the Internet, wireless communication, digital media, and online social networking tools.

But how exactly has globalization accelerated in these last three decades? Why does what has been happening justify the creation of a buzzword that not only captured the public imagination, but has also elicited conflicting emotional responses? Is contemporary globalization a 'good' or a 'bad' thing? Throughout this book we will consider possible answers to these crucial questions. In doing so, we will limit the application of the term 'globalization' to the contemporary period while keeping in mind that the forces driving these processes actually can be traced back thousands of years.

Before we embark on this next stage of our journey, let us pause and recall an important point we made in Chapter 1. Globalization is not a single process but a set of processes that operate simultaneously and unevenly on several levels and in various dimensions. We could compare these interactions and interdependencies to an intricate tapestry of overlapping shapes and colours. Yet, just as an auto mechanic apprentice must turn off and disassemble the car engine in order to understand its operation, so must the student of globalization apply analytical distinctions in order to make sense of the web of global connectivity. In ensuing chapters we will identify, explore, and assess patterns of globalization in each of its main domains—economic, political, cultural, ecological, and ideological—while keeping in mind its operation as an interacting whole on all geographical scales. Although we will study the various dimensions of globalization in isolation, we will resist the temptation to reduce globalization to a single 'most important' aspect. Thus will we avoid the blunder that kept the blind men from appreciating the full nature of the elephant.

Chapter 3
The economic dimension of globalization

At the beginning of the previous chapter we noted that new forms of technology centred on the Internet are one of the hallmarks of contemporary globalization. Indeed, technological progress of the magnitude seen in the last three decades is a good indicator for the occurrence of profound social transformations centred on the market. Changes in the way in which people undertake economic production and organize the exchange of commodities represent one obvious aspect of the great transformation of our age. Economic globalization refers to the intensification and stretching of economic connections across the globe. Gigantic flows of capital mediated by digital technology have stimulated trade in goods and services. Extending their reach around the world, markets have migrated to cyberspace and created new linkages among national and regional economies. Huge transnational corporations, powerful international economic institutions, and gigantic regional trading systems like Asian Pacific Economic Cooperation (APEC) or the European Union (EU) have emerged as the major building blocks of the 21st century's global economic order.

The emergence of the global economic order

Contemporary economic globalization can be traced back to the gradual emergence of a new international economic order assembled at an economic conference held towards the end of World War II in the sleepy New England town of Bretton Woods (see Illustration 6). Under the leadership of the United States of America and Great Britain, the major economic powers of the global North reversed their protectionist policies of the interwar period (1918–39). In addition to arriving at a firm commitment to expand international trade, the participants of the conference also agreed to establish binding rules on international economic activities. Moreover, they resolved to create a more stable money exchange system in which the value of each country's currency was pegged to a fixed gold value of the US dollar. Within these prescribed limits, individual nations were free to control the permeability of their borders. This allowed states to set their own political and economic agendas.

6. **Bretton Woods Conference of 1944**

Bretton Woods also set the institutional foundations for the establishment of three new international economic organizations. The International Monetary Fund (IMF) was created to administer the international monetary system. The International Bank for Reconstruction and Development, later known as the World Bank, was initially designed to provide loans for Europe's postwar reconstruction. During the 1950s, however, its purpose was expanded to fund various industrial projects in developing countries around the world. Finally, the General Agreement on Tariffs and Trade (GATT) was established in 1947 as a global trade organization charged with fashioning and enforcing multilateral trade agreements. In 1995, the World Trade Organization (WTO) was founded as the successor organization to GATT. By the late 1990s, the WTO had become the focal point of intense public controversy over the design and the effects of economic globalization.

In operation for almost three decades, the Bretton Woods regime contributed greatly to the establishment of what some observers have called the 'golden age of controlled capitalism'. Even the most conservative political parties in Europe and the United States embraced some version of state interventionism propagated by British economist John Maynard Keynes, the architect of the Bretton Woods system. Existing mechanisms of state control over international capital movements made possible full employment and the expansion of the welfare state. Rising wages and increased social services secured in the wealthy countries of the global North a temporary class compromise. By the early 1970s, however, the Bretton Woods system collapsed. Its demise strengthened those integrationist economic tendencies that later commentators would identify as the birth pangs of the new global economic order. What happened?

In response to profound political changes in the world that were undermining the economic competitiveness of US-based industries, President Richard Nixon abandoned the gold-based fixed rate system in 1971. The ensuing decade was characterized by global economic instability in the form of high inflation, low economic growth, high unemployment, public sector deficits, and two unprecedented energy crises due to Organization of Petroleum Exporting Countries (OPEC)'s ability to control a large part of the world's oil supply. Political forces in the global North most closely identified with the model of controlled capitalism suffered a series of spectacular election defeats at the hands of conservative political parties who advocated what came to be called a 'neoliberal' approach to economic and social policy.

In the 1980s, British Prime Minister Margaret Thatcher and US President Ronald Reagan acted as the co-leaders of the neoliberal revolution against Keynesianism. Soon thereafter, business elites in the US and Japan consciously linked the novel term 'globalization' to a political agenda aiming at the 'liberation' of state-regulated economies around the world.

> Neoliberalism is rooted in the classical liberal ideals of Adam Smith (1723–90) and David Ricardo (1772–1823), both of whom viewed the market as a self-regulating mechanism tending toward equilibrium of supply and demand, thus securing the most efficient allocation of resources. These British philosophers considered that any constraint on free competition would interfere with the natural efficiency of market mechanisms, inevitably leading to social stagnation, political corruption, and the creation of unresponsive state bureaucracies. They also advocated the elimination of tariffs on imports and other barriers to trade and capital flows between nations. British sociologist Herbert Spencer (1820–1903) added to this doctrine a twist of social Darwinism by arguing that free market economies constitute the most civilized form of human competition in which the 'fittest' would naturally rise to the top.

This budding neoliberal economic order received further legitimation with the 1989–91 collapse of communism in the Eastern Europe and the Soviet Union.

Since then, the three most significant developments related to economic globalization have been the internationalization of trade and finance, the increasing power of transnational corporations and large investment banks, and the enhanced role of international economic institutions like the IMF, the World Bank, and the WTO. Let us briefly examine these important features.

The internationalization of trade and finance

Many people associate economic globalization with the controversial issue of free trade. After all, the total value of world trade exploded from $57 billion in 1947 to an astonishing $14.9 trillion in 2010. In that year, China, the world's leading manufacturer, was responsible for 11 per cent of global exports while the US, the world's most voracious consumer, accounted for 13 per cent of global imports.

Indeed, the public debate over the alleged benefits and drawbacks of free trade still rages at a feverish pitch as wealthy Northern countries and regional trading blocs have increased their efforts to establish a single global market through far-reaching trade-liberalization agreements. While admitting that these new sets of trade rules often override national legislation, free trade proponents have nonetheless assured the public that the elimination or reduction of existing trade barriers among nations will increase global wealth and enhance consumer choice. The ultimate benefit of integrated markets, they argue, would be secure peaceful international relations and technological innovation for the benefit of all.

Concrete neoliberal measures

1. Privatization of public enterprises.
2. Deregulation of the economy.
3. Liberalization of trade and industry.
4. Massive tax cuts.
5. 'Monetarist' measures to keep inflation in check, even at the risk of increasing unemployment.
6. Strict control on organized labour.
7. The reduction of public expenditures, particularly social spending.
8. The down-sizing of government.
9. The expansion of international markets.
10. The removal of controls on global financial flows.

To be sure, there is evidence that some national economies have increased their productivity as a result of free trade. Millions of people have been lifted out of poverty in developing countries like China, India, or Indonesia. A 2012 World Bank report shows that for the first time the proportion of people living in extreme poverty—on less than $1.25 a day—fell in every developing region from 2005 to 2008. The progress has been so drastic that the United Nations' Millennium Goals to cut extreme poverty in half has been met three years before its 2015 deadline. Moreover, there are some clear material benefits that accrue to societies through specialization, competition, and the spread of technology. But it is less clear whether the profits resulting from free trade have been distributed fairly within and among populations. A number of studies suggest that the gap between rich and poor countries is actually widening at a fairly rapid pace (see Figure B).

The internationalization of trade has gone hand in hand with the liberalization of financial transactions. Its key components include the deregulation of interest rates, the removal of credit controls, the privatization of government-owned banks and financial institutions, and the explosive growth of investment banking. Globalization of financial trading allows for increased mobility among different segments of the financial industry, with fewer restrictions and greater investment opportunities. This new financial infrastructure emerged in the 1980s with the gradual deregulation of capital and securities markets in Europe, the Americas, East Asia, Australia, and New Zealand (see Figure C). A decade later, Southeast Asian countries, India, and several African nations followed suit. During the 1990s, new satellite systems and fibre-optic cables provided the nervous system of Internet-based technologies that further accelerated the liberalization of financial transactions. As captured by the snazzy title of Microsoft Chief Executive Officer (CEO) Bill Gates' best-selling book, many people conducted *business@the-speed-of-thought*. Millions of individual investors utilized global electronic investment networks not only to place their orders, but also to receive valuable information about relevant economic and political developments. In 2005, internet publishing, broadcasting and marketing firms traded approximately US$10 trillion in the United States alone. In early 2007, just before the Global Financial Crisis (GFC) hit, NASDAQ attempted to take over the London Stock Exchange, offering US$5.3 billion, a move that was rejected by the vast majority of shareholders in the London Stock Exchange.

Yet, a large part of the money involved in this 'financialization' of global capitalism has little to do with supplying capital for such productive investments as putting together machines or organizing raw materials and employees to produce saleable commodities. Most of the financial growth has occurred in the form of high-risk 'hedge funds' and other purely money-dealing currency and securities markets that trade claims to draw profits from future production. In other words, investors are betting on commodities or currency rates that do not yet exist. For example, in 2010, the

Total external debt of emerging and developing economies in 1970	US$70.2 billion
Total external debt of emerging and developing economies in 1980	US$569 billion
Total external debt of emerging and developing economies in 2013	US$6.857 trillion
Total external debt of emerging and developing economies in 2013 as a percentage of the total GDP	23.55%
Total external debt of emerging and developing economies in 2013 as a percentage of export goods and services	72.25%
Cost of the war in Iraq and Afghanistan to the USA (2001–2012)	US$1.349 trillion
Cost to convert one billion households to renewable wind energy	US$1.2 trillion
Amount Sudan owes the UK for loans (which were taken out by dictator Gaafar Nimeiry in 1984 for Cold War expenses)	US$1.055 billion
Percentage of this debt that is interest	75%
Amount the G8 promised to write off	US$100 billion
Amount of debt actually written off	US$46 billion
Number of countries eligible for the international Heavily Indebted Poor Countries initiative (HIPC)	32
Proportion of bilateral debt that the G8 counties have promised to cancel for the 42 HIPCs	100%
Proportion of multilateral debt that the World Bank and IMF will eventually cancel for the 42 HIPCs	65% (approx.)
Total amount of multilateral debt owned by the 42 HIPCs that is NOT eligible for cancellation	US$93 billion
Debt acquired by Indonesia under Suharto's brutal 30-year reign	US$150 billion

Amount stolen by Suharto over this time	US$48 billion
Percentage of Lebanon's GDP spent on debt servicing	19%
Percentage of Lebanon's GDP spent on public health	4%
Mozambique's gross debt in 2012	US$6.18 billion
Mozambique's predicted gross debt in 2017	US$13.43 billion
Google's net profit in 2011	US$9.74 billion

B. The global South: a fate worse than debt

Sources: IMF, <http://www.imf.org/external/pubs/ft/weo/2012/01/weodata/index.aspx>; CostofWar.com, 2012, <http://costofwar.com/>; Simon Murphy, 'Third of Debts Owed by Poor Countries to UK is Interest on Original Loans', *The Guardian*, 2012, <http://www.guardian.co.uk/world/2012/jan/22/poor-countries-debt-uk-interest>; Jubilee Campaign UK, *Getting into Debt*, 2010, p. 8: <http://www.jubileedebtcampaign.org.uk/download.php?id=992>

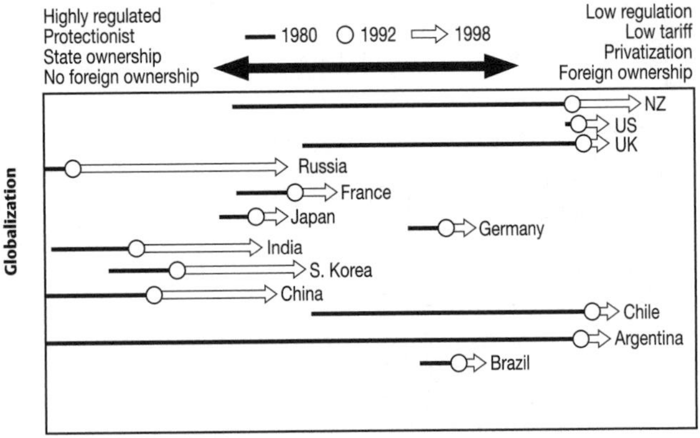

C. The advance of deregulation and liberalization, 1980–98

Source: Vincent Cable, *Globalization and Global Governance* (The Royal Institute of International Affairs, 1999), p. 20

equivalent of US$4 trillion was exchanged daily in global currency markets alone (see Illustration 7). Dominated by highly sensitive stock markets that drive high-risk innovation, the world's financial systems have become characterized by extremely high volatility, rampant competition, and general insecurity. Global speculators often take advantage of weak financial and banking regulations to make astronomical profits in emerging markets of developing countries. However, since these international capital flows can be reversed swiftly, they are capable of creating artificial boom-and-bust cycles that endanger the social welfare of entire regions.

In early 2008, this increasing volatility of financial flows combined with two decades of neoliberal deregulation to produce the GFC—the most serious economic crisis since the Great Depression of the 1930s. Before we continue our exploration of economic globalization with respect to the increasing power of transnational corporations and the enhanced role of international economic institutions, let us pause for a moment to examine briefly the causes and evolution of this crisis.

7. The New York Stock Exchange. Billions of shares change hands on an average trading day

The Global Financial Crisis

The possible negative consequences of a deregulated global financial infrastructure were already visible in the 1997–8 Southeast Asia Crisis. In the early 1990s, the governments of Thailand, Indonesia, Malaysia, South Korea, and the Philippines had gradually abandoned control over the domestic movement of capital in order to attract foreign direct investment. The ensuing influx of global investment translated into soaring stock and real estate markets all over Southeast Asia. But when those investors realized that prices had become inflated much beyond their actual value, they withdrew a total of US$105 billion from these countries. As a result, economic output fell, unemployment increased, and wages plummeted. By late 1997, the entire region found itself in the throes of a financial crisis that threatened to push the global economy into recession. This disastrous result was only narrowly averted by a combination of international bail-out packages and the immediate sale of Southeast Asian commercial assets to foreign corporate investors at rock-bottom prices.

A decade later, the world was not as lucky. The crash of 2008 has its roots in the 1980s and 1990s, when three successive US governments under Presidents Reagan, Bush I, and Clinton pushed for the significant deregulation of the domestic financial services industry. Perhaps the most important initiative in this regard was the 1999 repeal of the Glass-Steagall Act, which was signed into law by President Roosevelt in 1933 to prohibit commercial banks from engaging in investment activities on Wall Street. After all, the 1929 Crash and ensuing Great Depression had exposed the dangers of the savings and loan industry partaking in the speculative frenzy on Wall Street, which had ultimately led to the bankruptcy of many commercial banks and the loss of their customers' assets.

The neoliberal deregulation of US finance capital resulted in a frenzy of mergers that gave birth to huge financial-services conglomerates eager to plunge into securities ventures in areas that were not necessarily part of their underlying business. Derivatives, financial futures, credit default swaps, and other esoteric financial instruments became extremely popular when new computer-based mathematical models suggested more secure ways of managing the risk involved in buying an asset in the future at a price agreed to in the present. Relying far less on savings deposits, financial institutions borrowed from each other and sold these loans as securities, thus passing the risk on to investors in these securities. Other 'innovative' financial instruments such as 'hedge funds' leveraged with borrowed funds fuelled a variety of speculative activities. Billions of investment dollars flowed into complex 'residential mortgage-backed securities' that promised investors up to a 25 per cent return on equity.

Assured by monetarist policies aimed at keeping interest rates low and credit flowing, investment banks eventually expanded their search for capital by buying risky 'subprime' loans from mortgage brokers who, lured by the promise of big commissions, were accepting applications for housing mortgages with little or no down payment and without credit checks. Increasingly popular in the United States, most of these loans were adjustable-rate mortgages tied to fluctuations of short-term interest rates. Investment banks snapped up these high-risk loans knowing that they could resell these assets—and thus the risk involved—by bundling them into composite securities no longer subject to government regulation. Indeed, one of the most complex of these 'innovative' instruments of securitization—so-called 'collateralized debt obligations'—often hid the problematic loans by bundling them together with lower-risk assets and reselling them to unsuspecting investors.

But why, given the poor quality of collateral, did individual and institutional investors continue to buy these mortgage-backed securities? One can think of three principal reasons. First, as noted above, esoteric forms of securities often concealed the degree of risk involved, and investors failed to grasp the complexity of these new investment funds. Second, investors relied on the excellent reputation of such financial giants as Bank of America or Citicorp. Third, they trusted the positive credit ratings reports issued by Standard and Poor's or Moody's, failing to see how these firms were themselves implicated in the expanding speculative bubble. Seeking to maximize their profits, these credit ratings giants had a vested interest in the growth of securities markets and thus took an extremely rosy view of the inherent risks.

The high yields flowing from these new securities funds attracted more and more investors around the world, thus rapidly globalizing more than US$1 trillion worth of what came to be known as 'toxic assets'. In mid-2007, however, the financial steamroller finally ran out of fuel when seriously overvalued American real estate began to drop and foreclosures shot up dramatically. Investors finally realized the serious risks attached to the securities market and lost confidence. Consequently, the value of securitized mortgage funds fell and banks desperately, but in vain, tried to somehow eliminate the debts showing on their balance sheets.

Some of the largest and most venerable financial institutions, insurance companies, and government-sponsored underwriters of mortgages such as Lehman Brothers, Bear Stearns, Merrill Lynch, Goldman Sachs, AIG, Citicorp, J. P. Morgan Chase, IndyMac Bank, Morgan Stanley, Fannie Mae, and Freddie Mac—to name but a few—either declared bankruptcy or had to be bailed out by the US tax payer. Both the conservative Bush II and the liberal Obama administrations championed spending hundreds of billions of dollars on distressed mortgage securities in return for a government share in the businesses involved. Britain and most other industrialized countries followed suit with their own multi-billion dollar bailout packages, hoping that such massive injections of capital into ailing financial markets would help prop up financial institutions deemed 'too large to be allowed to fail'. But these generous rescue packages allowed large financial conglomerates to lose even more money without having to declare bankruptcy. The cost passed on to the world's taxpayers is truly staggering: future generations will have to repay trillions of dollars used for financing these bailout packages.

When reading about the GFC, huge numbers are splashed around very liberally. In spite of their similar spellings, million, billion, and trillion represent radically different orders of magnitude. Consider this hypothetical situation: If you spent US$1 every second, you would spend US$1 million in about twelve days. At the same rate, it would take you approximately thirty-two years to spend US$1 billion. Taking this to the next level, US$1 trillion would take you 31,546 years to spend!

However, one of the major consequences of the failing financial system was that banks trying to rebuild their capital base could hardly afford to keep lending large amounts of money. The flow of global credit froze to a trickle and businesses and individuals who relied on credit found it much more difficult to obtain. This credit shortage, in turn, impacted the profitability of many businesses, forcing them to cut back production and lay off workers. Industrial output declined, unemployment shot up as the world's stock markets dropped dramatically. By 2009, 14.3 trillion dollars, or 33 per cent of the value of the world's companies, was wiped out by the GFC. The developing world was especially hard hit with a financial shortfall of $700 billion by the end of 2010.

As the Global *Financial* Crisis solidified into a global *economic* crisis, Group of Twenty (G20) leaders met repeatedly to devise a common strategy to combat a global depression. (see Map 3). Although most countries were slowly pulling out of what came to be known as the 'Great Recession', economic growth between 2011 and 2013 in many parts of the world remained anaemic and unemployment numbers came down only very slowly. By 2011, it also became clear that the GFC and its ensuing global recession

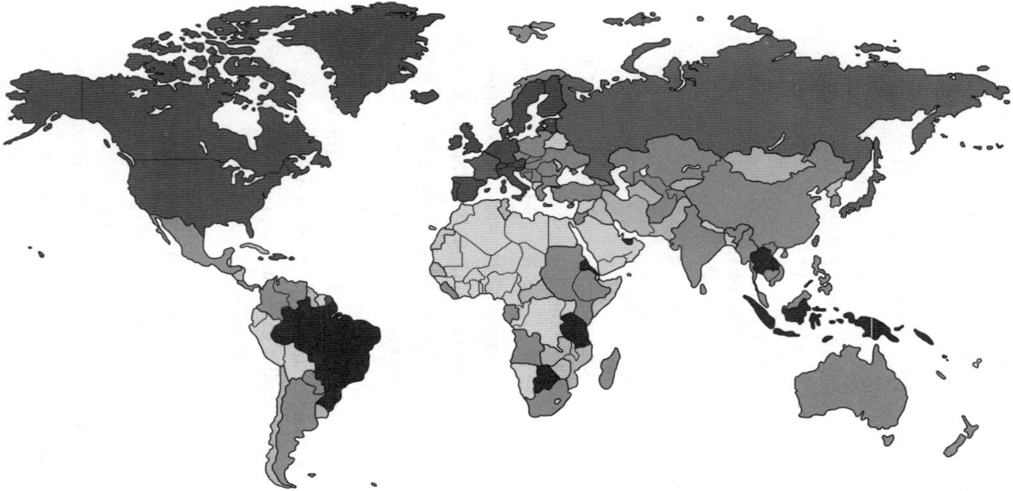

Map 3. Countries falling into recession as a result of the Global Financial Crisis, 2008

had spawned a severe sovereign debt crisis and a banking crisis, especially in the European Union. This rapidly escalating financial turmoil affecting first Greece, then Spain, and then other countries in the Eurozone continues to threaten the fragile recovery of the global economy. We will return to the impact of various 'global crises' on the future trajectory of globalization in the final chapter.

The power of transnational corporations

As we noted at the outset of this chapter, the increasing power of transnational corporations is another principal feature of economic globalization. Transnational corporations (TNCs) are the contemporary versions of the early modern commercial enterprises we discussed in the previous chapter. Powerful firms with subsidiaries in several countries, their numbers skyrocketed from 7,000 in 1970 to about 80,000 in 2012. Enterprises like General Motors, Wal-Mart, Exxon-Mobil, Mitsubishi, and Siemens belong to the 200 largest TNCs, which account for over half of the world's industrial output. None of these corporations maintains headquarters outside of North America, Mexico, Europe, China, Japan, and South Korea. This geographical concentration reflects existing asymmetrical power relations between the North and the South.

Rivalling nation-states in their economic power, these corporations control much of the world's investment capital, technology, and access to international markets. In order to maintain their prominent positions in the global marketplace, TNCs frequently merge with other corporations. Some of these recent mergers include the US$162 billion marriage of the world's largest Internet provider, AOL, with entertainment giant Time-Warner; the purchase of Chrysler Motors by Daimler-Benz for US$43 billion; and the US$115 billion merger between Sprint Corporation and MCI WorldCom. In 2007, global telecommunications TNCs Nokia and Siemens merged in a deal worth approximately US$38 million. In 2008, at the height of the GFC, Bank of America acquired Merrill Lynch for US$50 billion.

A 2009 comparison of gross domestic products (GDPs) and corporate sales reveals that forty-four of the world's hundred largest economies are corporations; fifty-six are countries. (see Figure D). Hence, it is not surprising that some critics have characterized economic globalization as 'corporate globalization' or 'globalization-from-above'.

TNCs have consolidated their global operations in an increasingly deregulated global labour market. The availability of cheap labour, resources, and favourable production conditions in the global South has enhanced corporate mobility and profitability. Accounting for over 70 per cent of world trade, TNCs have boosted their foreign direct investments by approximately 15 per cent annually. As the 2012 UNCTAD *World Investment Report* shows, the total foreign direct investment of the world's hundred largest TNCs in 2011 amounted to over US$374 billion. Their ability to disperse manufacturing processes into many discrete phases carried out in many different locations around the world reflects the changing nature of global production. Such transnational production networks allow TNCs like Wal-Mart, General Motors, and Volkswagen to produce, distribute, and market their products on a global scale.

No doubt, the growing power of TNCs has profoundly altered the structure and functioning of the international economy. These giant firms and their global strategies have become major determinants of trade flows, the location of industries, and other economic activities around the world.

A ground-breaking study published in 2011 analysed the relationships between 43,060 large TNCs in terms of share ownerships linking them. The findings revealed that a relatively small core of 1,318 corporations appeared to own collectively through their shares the majority of the world's large blue chip and manufacturing firms. In fact, an even smaller number of these TNCS—147 super-connected corporations to be exact—controlled

Corporation	Industry/ Headquarters	Revenue (US$m)	Country	GDP (US$m)
1 Royal Dutch Shell	Oil, Netherlands	470,171	Poland	469,440
2 Exxon Mobil	Oil, USA	452,926	Sweden	458,552
3 Wal-Mart Stores	Retail, USA	446,950	Saudi Arabia	434,666
4 Sinopec Corp.	Oil, China	398,088	Venezuela	391,847
5 BP	Oil, UK	375,517	South Africa	363,910
6 Vitol	Oil, Switzerland	297,000	United Arab Emirates	297,648
7 China National Petroleum Corporation	Oil, China	273,404	Colombia	299,886
8 Chevron Corporation	Oil, USA	245,621	Finland	238,041
9 ConocoPhillips	Oil, USA	237,272	Malaysia	237,797
10 Toyota Motors	Car, Japan	224,251	Egypt	218,894

D. Transnational corporations versus countries: a comparison

Sources: Forbes Fortune 500, 2012: <http://money.cnn.com/magazines/fortune/fortune500/2012/full_list/>; Shell, 2011, p. 10 <http://www.annualreportandform20f.shell.com/2011/servicepages/downloads/files/download2.php?file=entire_shell_20f_11.pdf>; BP, 2011, p. 58: <http://www.bp.com/annualreport>; Vitol, 2011, p. 2: <http://www.vitol.com/downloads/vitol-group-brochure-2012.pdf>; Sinopec, 2011, p. 5: <http://english.sinopec.com/download_center/reports/2012/20120326/download/2011AnnualReport.pdf>; Toyota, 2012, p. 2: <http://www.toyota-global.com/investors/financial_result/2012/pdf/q4/summary.pdf>; World Bank, 2012: <http://data.worldbank.org/indicator/NY.GDP.MKTP.CD?order=wbapi_data_value_2010%20wbapi_data_value%20wbapi_data_value-last&sort=desc>

40 per cent of the total wealth in the network. Most of them were financial institutions like Barclays Bank, which topped the list. Ironically, it was this very bank that found itself at the centre of a huge scandal that rocked the financial world in July 2012 when it was revealed that Barclays and fifteen other major banks had rigged the world's most important global interest rate for years. Indeed, TNCs have become extremely important players that influence the economic, political, and social welfare of many nations. Here is a final example.

The enhanced role of international economic institutions

The three international economic institutions most frequently mentioned in the context of economic globalization are the IMF, the World Bank, and the WTO. These three institutions enjoy the

Nokia's role in the Finnish economy

Named after a small town in southwest Finland, Nokia Corporation rose from modest beginnings nearly two decades ago to become the world's largest TNC engaged in the manufacturing of mobile phones and converging Internet industries. Its products connect more than a billion people in an invisible web around the globe. Employing over 100,000 people in 120 countries, Nokia amassed a global revenue of over US$50 billion in 2010, which translated into a profit of US$2.5 billion. However, Nokia's gift to Finland—the distinction of being the most interconnected nation in the world—came at the price of economic dependency. Nokia is the engine of Finland's economy, representing two-thirds of the stock market's value and one-fifth of the nation's total export. It employs 22,000 Finns, not counting the estimated 20,000 domestic employees who work for companies that depend on Nokia contracts. The corporation produces a large part of Finland's tax revenue, and its US$25 billion in annual sales almost equals the entire national budget. Yet, when Nokia's growth rate slowed in the wake of the GFC—10,000 employees were let go in 2012 and some Finnish factories shut down—company executives successfully pressured the Finnish government to reduce its corporate tax rates. Today, many Finnish citizens fear that such influence wielded by relatively few Nokia managers will translate into further tax concessions that might adversely affect the country's generous and egalitarian welfare system.

privileged position of making and enforcing the rules of a global economy that is sustained by significant power differentials between the global North and South. Since we will discuss the WTO in some detail in Chapter 8, let us focus here on the other two institutions. As pointed out above, the IMF and the World Bank emerged from the Bretton Woods system. During the Cold

War, their important function of providing loans for developing countries became connected to the West's political objective of containing communism. Starting in the 1970s, and especially after the fall of the Soviet Union, the economic agenda of the IMF and the World Bank has synchronized neoliberal interests to integrate and deregulate markets around the world.

In return for supplying much-needed loans to developing countries, the IMF and the World Bank demand from their creditor nations the implementation of so-called 'structural adjustment programmes'. Unleashed on developing countries in the 1990s, this set of neoliberal policies is often referred to as the 'Washington Consensus'. It was devised and codified by John Williamson, who was an IMF adviser in the 1970s. The various sections of the programme were mainly directed at countries with large foreign debts remaining from the 1970s and 1980s. The official purpose of the document was to reform the internal economic mechanisms of debtor countries in the developing world so that they would be in a better position to repay the debts they had incurred. In practice, however, the terms of the programme spelled out a new form of colonialism. The ten points of the Washington Consensus, as defined by Williamson, required governments to implement the following structural adjustments in order to qualify for loans:

1. A guarantee of fiscal discipline, and a curb to budget deficits.
2. A reduction of public expenditure, particularly in the military and public administration.
3. Tax reform, aiming at the creation of a system with a broad base and with effective enforcement.
4. Financial liberalization, with interest rates determined by the market.
5. Competitive exchange rates, to assist export-led growth.
6. Trade liberalization, coupled with the abolition of import licensing and a reduction of tariffs.
7. Promotion of foreign direct investment.

8. Privatization of state enterprises, leading to efficient management and improved performance.
9. Deregulation of the economy.
10. Protection of property rights.

It is no coincidence that this programme is called the 'Washington Consensus', for, from the outset, the United States has been the dominant power in the IMF and the World Bank. Unfortunately, however, large portions of the 'development loans' granted by these institutions have either been pocketed by authoritarian political leaders or have enriched local businesses and the Northern corporations they usually serve. Sometimes, exorbitant sums are spent on ill-considered construction projects. Most importantly, however, structural adjustment programmes rarely produce the desired result of 'developing' debtor societies, because mandated cuts in public spending translate into fewer social programmes, reduced educational opportunities, more environmental pollution, and greater poverty for the vast majority of people. Typically, the largest share of the national budget is spent on servicing outstanding debts. For example, in 2005, developing countries paid US$355,025.5 million in debt servicing, while receiving only US$80,534.1 million in aid. Pressured by anti-corporate globalist forces, the IMF and the World Bank were only recently willing to consider a new policy of blanket debt forgiveness in special cases. With the rise of China, however, some commentators have predicted the forging of a new 'Beijing Consensus' the institutional architecture of which might be quite different from the current US-dominated economic paradigm.

As this chapter has shown, economic perspectives on globalization can hardly be discussed apart from an analysis of political process and institutions. After all, the intensification of global economic interconnections does not simply fall from the sky; rather, it is set into motion by a series of political decisions. Hence, while acknowledging the importance of economics in our story of globalization, this chapter nonetheless ends with the suggestion that we ought to be sceptical of one-sided accounts that identify expanding economic activity as both the primary aspect of globalization and the engine behind its rapid development. The multidimensional nature of globalization demands that we flesh out in more detail the interaction between its political and economic aspects.

Chapter 4
The political dimension of globalization

Political globalization refers to the intensification and expansion of political interrelations across the globe. These processes raise an important set of political issues pertaining to the principle of state sovereignty, the growing impact of intergovernmental organizations, and the future prospects for regional and global governance, and environmental policies affecting our planet. Obviously, these themes respond to the evolution of political arrangements beyond the framework of the nation-state, thus breaking new conceptual and institutional ground. After all, for the last few centuries, humans have organized their political differences along territorial lines that generated a sense of 'belonging' to a particular nation-state.

This artificial division of planetary social space into 'domestic' and 'foreign' spheres corresponds to people's collective identities based on the creation of a common 'us' and an unfamiliar 'them'. Thus, the modern nation-state system has rested on psychological foundations and cultural assumptions that convey a sense of existential security and historical continuity, while at the same time demanding from its citizens that they put their national loyalties to the ultimate test. Nurtured by demonizing images of the Other, people's belief in the superiority of their own nation has supplied the mental energy required for large-scale warfare—just as the enormous productive capacities of the modern state have provided the material means necessary to fight the 'total wars' of the last century.

Contemporary manifestations of globalization have led to the partial permeation of these old territorial borders, in the process also softening hard conceptual boundaries and cultural lines of demarcation. Emphasizing these tendencies, commentators belonging to the camp of 'hyperglobalizers' have suggested that the period since the late 1960s has been marked by a radical 'deterritorialization' of politics, rule, and governance. Considering such pronouncements premature at best and erroneous at worst, 'globalization sceptics' have not only affirmed the continued relevance of the nation-state as the political container of modern social life but have also pointed to the emergence of regional blocs as evidence for new forms of territorialization. Some of these critics have gone so far as to suggest that globalization is actually accentuating people's sense of nationality. As each group of global studies scholars presents different assessments of the fate of the modern nation-state, they also quarrel over the relative importance of political and economic factors.

Out of these disagreements there have emerged three fundamental questions that probe the extent of political globalization. First, is it really true that the power of the nation-state has been curtailed by massive flows of capital, people, and technology across territorial boundaries? Second, are the primary causes of these flows to be found in politics or in economics? Third, are we witnessing the emergence of new global governance structures? Before we respond to these questions in more detail, let us briefly consider the main features of the modern nation-state system.

The modern nation-state system

The origins of the modern nation-state system can be traced back to 17th-century political developments in Europe. In 1648, the Peace of Westphalia concluded a series of religious wars among the main European powers following the Protestant Reformation. Based on the newly formulated principles of sovereignty and territoriality, the ensuing model of self-contained, impersonal states challenged the medieval mosaic of small polities in which political power tended to be local and personal in focus but still subordinated to a larger imperial authority. While the emergence of the Westphalian model did not eclipse the transnational character of vast imperial domains overnight, it nonetheless gradually strengthened a new conception of international law based on the principle that all states had an equal right to self-determination. Whether ruled by absolutist kings in France and Prussia or in a more democratic fashion by the constitutional monarchs and republican leaders of England and the Netherlands, these unified territorial areas constituted the foundation for modernity's secular and national system of political power. According to political scientist David Held, the Westphalian model contained the following essential points:

1. The world consists of, and is divided into, sovereign territorial states which recognize no superior authority.
2. The processes of law-making, the settlement of disputes, and law enforcement are largely in the hands of individual states.
3. International law is oriented to the establishment of minimal rules of co-existence; the creation of enduring relationships is an aim, but only to the extent that it allows state objectives to be met.
4. Responsibility for cross-border wrongful acts is a 'private matter' concerning only those affected.
5. All states are regarded as equal before the law, but legal rules do not take account of asymmetries of power.
6. Differences among states are often settled by force; the principle of effective power holds sway. Virtually no legal fetters exist to curb the resort to force; international legal standards afford only minimal protection.
7. The collective priority of all states should be to minimize the impediments to state freedom.

The centuries following the Peace of Westphalia saw the further centralization of political power, the expansion of state administration, the development of professional diplomacy, and the successful monopolization of the means of coercion in the hands of the state. Moreover, states also provided the military means required for the expansion of commerce, which, in turn, contributed to the spread of this European form of political rule around the globe.

The modern nation-state system found its mature expression at the end of World War I in US President Woodrow Wilson's famous 'Fourteen Points' based on the principle of national self-determination. But his assumption that all forms of national identity should be given their territorial expression in a sovereign 'nation-state' proved to be extremely difficult to enforce in practice. Moreover, by enshrining the nation-state as the ethical and legal pinnacle of his proposed interstate system, Wilson unwittingly lent some legitimacy to those radical ethnonationalist forces that pushed the world's main powers into another war of global proportions.

Yet, President Wilson's commitment to the nation-state coexisted with his internationalist dream of establishing a global system of collective security under the auspices of a new international organization, the League of Nations. His idea of giving international cooperation an institutional expression was eventually realized with the founding of the United Nations in 1945. While deeply rooted in a political order based on the modern nation-state system, the UN and other fledgling intergovernmental organizations also served as catalysts for the gradual extension of political activities across national boundaries, thus undermining the principle of national sovereignty.

As globalization tendencies grew stronger during the 1970s, it became clear that the international society of separate states was rapidly turning into a global web of political interdependencies

8. The Security Council of the United Nations in session. The Council is comprised of 15 states, five of which—the USA, the UK, France, Russia, and China—are permanent members. According to Article 25 of the UN Charter, member nations must comply with Security Council resolutions

that challenged conventional forms of national sovereignty. In 1990, at the outset of the Gulf War, US President George H. W. Bush effectively pronounced dead the Westphalian model by announcing the birth of a 'new world order' whose leaders no longer respected the idea that cross-border wrongful acts were a matter concerning only those states affected. Did this mean that the modern nation-state system was no longer viable?

The demise of the nation-state?

Hyperglobalizers respond to the above question affirmatively. At the same time, most of them consider political globalization a mere secondary phenomenon driven by more fundamental economic and technological forces. They argue that politics has been rendered almost powerless by an unstoppable techno-economic juggernaut that will crush all governmental attempts to reintroduce restrictive policies and regulations. Endowing economics with an inner logic apart from, and superior to, politics, these commentators look forward to a new phase in world history in which the main role of government will be to serve as a superconductor for global capitalism.

Pronouncing the rise of a 'borderless world', hyperglobalizers seek to convince the public that globalization inevitably involves the decline of bounded territory as a meaningful concept for understanding political and social change. Consequently, this group of commentators suggests that political power is located in global social formations and expressed through global networks rather than through territorially based states. In fact, they argue that nation-states have already lost their dominant role in the global economy. As territorial divisions are becoming increasingly irrelevant, states are even less capable of determining the direction of social life within their borders. For example, since the workings of genuinely global capital markets dwarf their ability to control exchange rates or protect their currency, nation-states have become vulnerable to the discipline imposed by economic choices made elsewhere, over which states have no practical control. Hyperglobalizers insist that the minimalist political order of the future will be determined by regional economies linked together in an almost seamless global web of production and exchange.

The group of globalization sceptics disagrees, highlighting instead the central role of politics in unleashing the forces of globalization, especially through the successful mobilization of political power. In their view, the rapid expansion of global economic activity can be reduced neither to a natural law of the market nor to the development of computer technology. Rather, it originated with political decisions to lift international restrictions on capital made by neoliberal governments in the 1980s and 1990s. Once those decisions were implemented, global markets and new technologies came into their own. The clear implication of this perspective is that territory still matters. Hence, globalization sceptics insist on the continued relevance of conventional political units, operating either in the form of modern nation-states or global cities.

The arguments of both hyperglobalizers and sceptics remain entangled in a particularly vexing version of the chicken-and-the-egg problem. After all, economic forms of interdependence are set into motion by political decisions, but these decisions are nonetheless made in particular economic contexts. As we have noted in previous chapters, the economic and political aspects of globalization are profoundly interconnected. There is no question that recent economic developments such as trade liberalization and deregulation have significantly constrained the set of political options open to states, particularly in the global South. For example, it has become much easier for capital to escape taxation and other national policy restrictions. Thus, global markets frequently undermine the capacity of governments to set independent national policy objectives and impose their own domestic standards. Hence, we ought to acknowledge the decline of the nation-state as a sovereign entity and the ensuing devolution of state power to regional and local governments as well as to various supranational institutions.

On the other hand, such a concession does not necessarily mean that nation-states have become impotent bystanders to the workings of global forces. Governments can still take measures to make their economies more or less attractive to global investors. In addition, nation-states have retained control over education, infrastructure, and, most importantly, population movements. Indeed, immigration control, together with population registration and monitoring, has often been cited as the most notable exception to the general trend toward global integration. Although only 2 per cent of the world's population live outside their country of origin, immigration control has become a central issue in most advanced nations. Many governments seek to restrict population flows, particularly those originating in the poor countries of the global South. Even in the United States, annual inflows of about 1,400,000 immigrants during the 2000s only equalled the levels recorded during the first two decades of the 20th century.

Finally, the series of drastic national security measures that were implemented worldwide as a response to the terrorist attacks of 9/11 reflect political dynamics that run counter to the hyperglobalizers' predictions of a borderless world. Some civil rights advocates still fear that the enormous expansion of national security measures around the world might enable states to re-impose restrictions on the freedom of movement and assembly. At the same time, however, the activities of global terrorist networks have revealed the inadequacy of conventional national security structures based on the modern nation-state system, thus forcing national governments to engage in new forms of international cooperation.

Overall, then, we ought to reject premature pronouncements of the impending demise of the nation-state while acknowledging its increasing difficulties in performing some of its traditional functions. Contemporary globalization has weakened some of the conventional boundaries between domestic and foreign policies while fostering the growth of supraterritorial social spaces and institutions that, in turn, unsettle traditional political arrangements. In the second decade of the 21st century, the world finds itself in a transitional phase between the modern nation-state system and postmodern forms of global governance.

Political globalization and global governance

Political globalization is most visible in the rise of supraterritorial institutions and associations held together by common norms and interests. In this early phase of global governance, these structures resemble an eclectic network of interrelated power centres such as municipal and provincial authorities, regional blocs, international organizations, and national and international private-sector associations.

On the municipal and provincial level, there has been a remarkable growth in the number of policy initiatives and transborder links between various sub-state authorities. For example, Chinese provinces and US federal states have established permanent missions and points of contact, some of which operate relatively autonomously with little oversight from their respective national governments. Various provinces and federal states in Canada, India, and Brazil are developing their own trade agendas and financial strategies to obtain loans. An example of international cooperation on the municipal level is the rise of powerful city networks like the World Association of Major Metropolises that develop cooperative ventures to deal with common local issues across national borders. 'Global Cities'

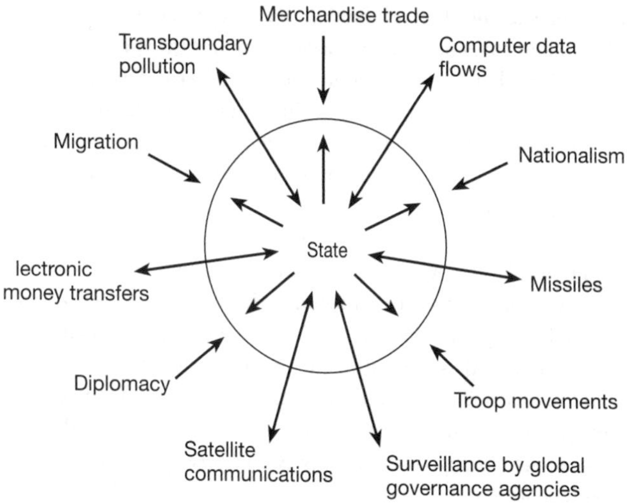

E. The nation-state in a globalizing world

Source: Jan Aart Scholte, 'The globalization of world politics', in John Baylis and Steve Smith (eds.), *The Globalization of World Politics*, 2nd edn. (Oxford University Press, 2001), p. 22

like Tokyo, London, New York, and Singapore tend to be more closely connected to each other than they are to many cities in their home countries.

On the regional level, there has been an extraordinary proliferation of multilateral organizations and agreements. Regional clubs and agencies have sprung up across the world, leading some observers to speculate that they will eventually replace nation-states as the basic unit of governance. Starting out as attempts to integrate regional economies, these regional blocs have, in some cases, already evolved into loose political federations with common institutions of governance. For example, the European Community began in 1950 with French Foreign Minister Robert Schuman's modest plan to create a supranational institution charged with regulating French and

German coal and steel production. Half a century later, 15 member states have formed a close community with political institutions that create common public policies and design binding security arrangements. Following the dissolution of the Soviet Union in 1991, many of the formerly communist countries in Eastern Europe have submitted their formal accession applications to the EU.

On a global level, governments have formed a number of international organizations, including the UN, NATO, WTO, and OECD. Full legal membership of these organizations is open to states only, and the decision-making authority lies with representatives from national governments. The proliferation of these transnational bodies has shown that nation-states find it increasingly difficult to manage sprawling networks of social interdependence.

Finally, the emerging structure of global governance shaped by 'global civil society', a realm populated by thousands of voluntary, non-governmental associations of worldwide reach. International NGOs like Doctors Without Borders or Greenpeace represent millions of ordinary citizens who are prepared to challenge political and economic decisions made by nation-states and intergovernmental organizations. We will examine the 'justice-globalist' activities of some of these organizations in Chapter 7.

Some globalization researchers believe that political globalization might facilitate the emergence of democratic transnational social forces anchored in this thriving sphere of global civil society. Predicting that democratic rights will ultimately become detached from their narrow relationship to discrete territorial units, these optimistic voices anticipate the creation of a democratic global governance structure based on Western cosmopolitan ideals, international legal arrangements, and a web of expanding linkages

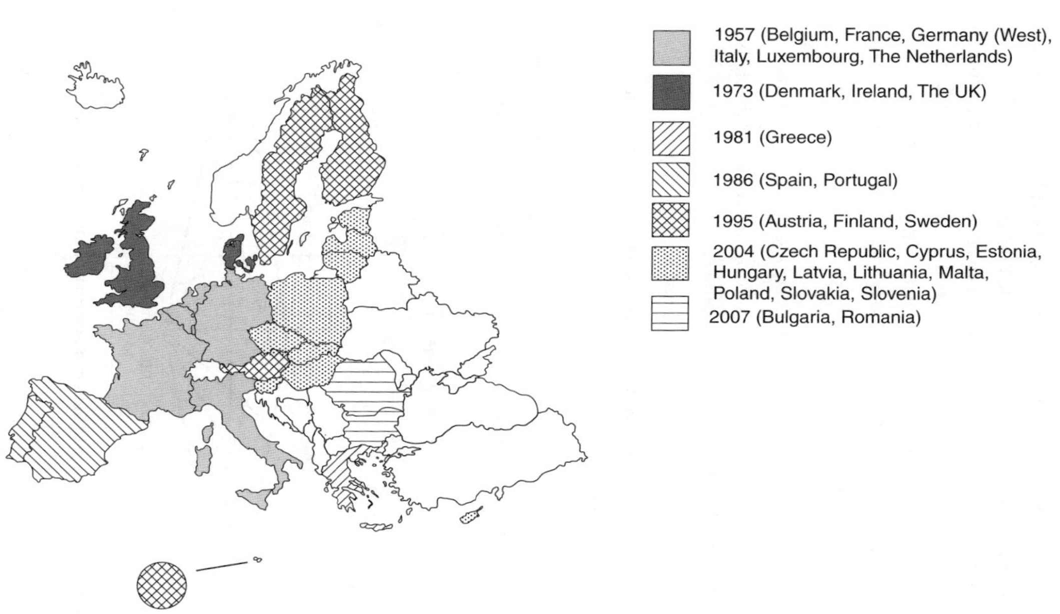
1957 (Belgium, France, Germany (West), Italy, Luxembourg, The Netherlands)
1973 (Denmark, Ireland, The UK)
1981 (Greece)
1986 (Spain, Portugal)
1995 (Austria, Finland, Sweden)
2004 (Czech Republic, Cyprus, Estonia, Hungary, Latvia, Lithuania, Malta, Poland, Slovakia, Slovenia)
2007 (Bulgaria, Romania)

Map 4. The European Union

between various governmental and non-governmental organizations. If such a promising scenario indeed will come to pass, then the final outcome of political globalization might well be the emergence of a cosmopolitan democracy that would constitute the basis for a plurality of identities flourishing within a structure of mutual toleration and accountability. According to David Held, one of the chief proponents of this view, the cosmopolitan democracy of the future would contain the following political features:

1. A global parliament connected to regions, states, and localities;
2. A new charter of rights and duties locked into different domains of political, social, and economic power;
3. The formal separation of political and economic interests;
4. An interconnected global legal system with mechanisms of enforcement from the local to the global.

A number of less optimistic commentators have challenged the idea that political globalization is moving in the direction of

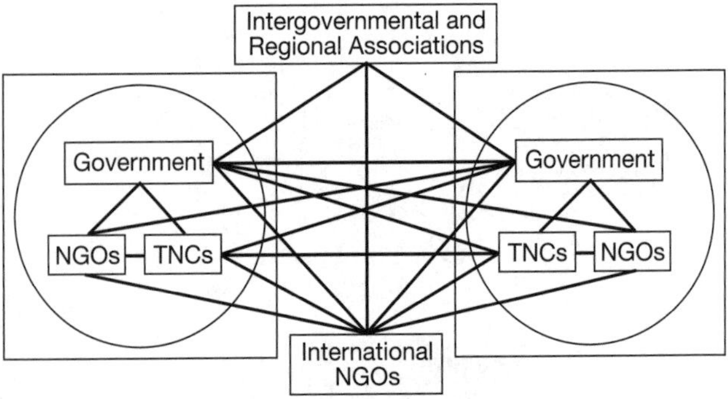

F. Incipient global governance: a network of interrelated power centres

Source: adapted from Peter Willets, 'Transnational actors and international organizations in global politics', in Baylis and Smith, *The Globalization of World Politics*, 5th edition, 2011, p. 339

cosmopolitan democracy. Most criticisms boil down to the charge that such a vision indulges in an abstract idealism that fails to engage current political developments on the level of public policy. Sceptics have also expressed the suspicion that the proponents of cosmopolitanism do not consider in sufficient detail the cultural feasibility of global democracy. In other words, the worldwide intensification of cultural, political, and economic interaction makes the possibility of resistance and opposition just as real as the benign vision of mutual accommodation and tolerance of differences. To follow up on this cultural dimension of globalization, let us turn to the next chapter.

Chapter 5
The cultural dimension of globalization

As our opening discussion of the 2010 Football World Cup has shown, even a *very short* introduction to globalization would be woefully inadequate without an examination of its cultural dimension. Cultural globalization refers to the intensification and expansion of cultural flows across the globe. Obviously, 'culture' is a very broad concept; it is frequently used to describe the whole of human experience. In order to avoid the ensuing problem of overgeneralization, it is important to make analytical distinctions between aspects of social life. For example, we associate the adjective 'economic' with the production, exchange, and consumption of commodities. If we are discussing the 'political', we mean practices related to the generation and distribution of power in societies. If we are talking about the 'cultural', we are concerned with the symbolic construction, articulation, and dissemination of meaning. Given that language, music, and images constitute the major forms of symbolic expression, they assume special significance in the sphere of culture.

The exploding network of cultural interconnections and interdependencies in the last decades has led some commentators to suggest that cultural practices lie at the very heart of contemporary globalization. Yet, cultural globalization did not start with the worldwide dissemination of rock 'n' roll, Coca-Cola, or football. As noted in Chapter 2, expansive civilizational exchanges are much older than modernity. Still, the volume and extent of cultural transmissions in the contemporary period have far exceeded those of earlier eras. Facilitated by the Internet and our proliferating mobile digital devices, the dominant symbolic systems of meaning of our age—such as individualism, consumerism, and various religious discourses—circulate more freely and widely than ever before. As images and ideas can be more easily and rapidly transmitted from one place to another, they profoundly impact the way people experience their everyday lives. Today, cultural practices have escaped fixed localities such as town and nation, eventually acquiring new meanings in interaction with dominant global themes.

The thematic landscape traversed by scholars of cultural globalization is vast and the questions they raise are too numerous to be fleshed out in this short introduction. Rather than offering a long laundry list of relevant topics, this chapter will focus on three important themes: the tension between sameness and difference in the emerging global culture; the crucial role of transnational media corporations in disseminating popular culture; and the globalization of languages.

Global culture: sameness or difference?

Does globalization make people around the world more alike or more different? This is the question most frequently raised in discussions on the subject of cultural globalization. A group of commentators we might call 'pessimistic' hyperglobalizers argue in favour of the former. They suggest that we are not moving towards a cultural rainbow that reflects the diversity of the world's existing cultures. Rather, we are witnessing the rise of an increasingly homogenized popular culture underwritten by a Western 'culture industry' based in New York, Hollywood, London, and Milan. As evidence for their interpretation, these commentators point to Amazonian Indians wearing Nike training shoes; denizens of the Southern Sahara purchasing Yankees baseball caps; and Palestinian youths proudly displaying their Chicago Bulls sweatshirts in downtown Ramallah. Referring to the diffusion of Anglo-American values and consumer goods as the 'Americanization of the world', the proponents of this cultural homogenization thesis argue that Western norms and lifestyles are overwhelming more vulnerable cultures. Although there have been serious attempts by some countries to resist these forces of 'cultural imperialism'—for example, a ban on satellite dishes in Iran, and the French imposition of tariffs and quotas on imported film and television—the spread of American popular culture seems to be unstoppable.

But these manifestations of sameness are also evident inside the dominant countries of the global North. American sociologist George Ritzer coined the term 'McDonaldization' to describe the wide-ranging sociocultural processes by which the principles of the fast-food restaurant are coming to dominate more and more sectors of American society as well as the rest of the world. On the surface, these principles appear to be rational in their attempts to offer efficient and predictable ways of serving people's needs. However, looking behind the façade of repetitive TV commercials that claim to 'love to see you smile', we can identify a number of serious problems. For one, the generally low nutritional value of fast-food meals—and particularly their high fat content—has been implicated in the rise of serious health problems such as heart disease, diabetes, cancer, and juvenile obesity. Moreover, the impersonal, routine operations of 'rational' fast-service establishments actually undermine expressions of forms of cultural diversity. In the long run, the McDonaldization of the world amounts to the imposition of uniform standards that eclipse human creativity and dehumanize social relations (see Figure G).

One particular thoughtful analyst in this group of pessimistic hyperglobalizers is American political theorist Benjamin Barber. In his popular book *Consumed* (2007), he warns his readers against an 'ethos of infantilization' that sustains global capitalism, turning adults into children through dumbed down advertising and consumer goods while also targeting children as consumers. This ethos is premised on the recognition that there is not an endless market for consumerist goods as was once thought. Global inequality contributes to stifling the growth of markets and of capitalism. In order to expand markets and make a profit, global capitalists are developing homogenous global products targeting the young and wealthy throughout the world, as well as turning children into consumers. Thus, global consumerism becomes increasingly soulless and unethical in its pursuit of profit.

Optimistic hyperglobalizers agree with their pessimistic colleagues that cultural globalization generates more sameness, but they consider this outcome to be a good thing. For example, American social theorist Francis Fukuyama explicitly welcomes the global spread of Anglo-American values and lifestyles, equating the Americanization of the world with the expansion of democracy and free markets (see Illustration 9). But optimistic hyperglobalizers do not just come in the form of American chauvinists who apply the old theme of manifest destiny to the global arena. Some representatives of this camp consider themselves staunch cosmopolitans who celebrate the Internet as the harbinger of a homogenized 'techno-culture'. Others are free-market enthusiasts who embrace the values of global consumer capitalism.

It is one thing to acknowledge the existence of powerful homogenizing tendencies in the world, but it is quite another to assert that the cultural diversity existing on our planet is destined to vanish. In fact, several influential commentators offer a contrary assessment that links globalization to new forms of cultural expression. Sociologist Roland Robertson, for example, contends that global cultural flows often reinvigorate local cultural niches. Hence, rather than being totally obliterated by the Western consumerist forces of sameness, local difference and

Average time Americans spend watching TV per week	34 hours
Average time Americans spend socializing per week	5 hours
Percentage of advertizing content that makes up one hour of prime time TV	36%
Number of advertisements, logos and labels seen by the average American every day	16,000
Percentage of Americans who regularly watch TV while eating dinner	66%
Percentage of adult Americans who are obese	35.7%
The percentage of the average American's daily vegetable intake that is made up of French fries	25%
Average annual intake of meat in the USA (vs. India)	100kg (5kg)
Average number of cows in a single fast-food hamburger patty	55–1,082
Average number of hamburgers eaten per week	3
Carbon dioxide produced to make one hamburger	3.6–6.1 kg CO_2
Carbon dioxide produced by the USA's hamburger consumption annually (more than Hungary's national CO_2 output)	65,250,000 metric tons CO_2
The number of other countries that contribute ingredients to the average American meal	5

The number of cars registered in the USA (2010)	250,272,812
Amount of rubbish produced by Americans in 2010	226 million tonnes
Total mass of living humans on Earth	287 million tonnes
Percentage of Americans who believe that God created humans in their present form less than 10,000 years ago	46%

G. The American way of life

Sources: G. C. Smith, K. E. Belk, J. A. Scanga, J. N. Sofos, and J. D. Tatum. 2002. 'Traceback, Traceability and Source Verification in the U.S. Beef Industry'. Proceedings of the IX Simposio Centroamericano y del Caribe Sobre Procesamiento de Carnes, Cartago, Costa Rica. pp. 21–32; Leopold Center for Sustainable Agriculture, 2003, 'Checking the food odometer: Comparing food miles for local versus conventional produce sales to Iowa institutions', p. 1: <http://www.leopold.iastate.edu/sites/default/files/pubs-and-papers/2003-07-checking-food-odometer-comparing-food-miles-local-versus-conventional-produce-sales-iowa-institution.pdf>; Centre for Disease Control and Prevention, 2012: <http://www.cdc.gov/obesity/data/adult.html>; Jamais Cascio, *The Cheeseburger Footprint*, 2012, <http://www.openthefuture.com/cheeseburger_CF.html>; Nielsen, *State of the Media: Cross Platform Report*, 2011, <http://www.nielsen.com/content/dam/corporate/us/en/reports-downloads/2012-Reports/nielsen-cross-platform-q4-2011.pdf>; Bureau of Labor Statistics, 2012, <http://www.bls.gov/news.release/atus.nr0.htm>; Dharma Singh Khalsa, *Brain Longevity*, Grand Central Publishing, p. 29; Norman Herr, *The Sourcebook for Teaching Science*, 2012 <http://www.csun.edu/science/health/docs/tv&health.html>; Bureau of Transport Statistics, 2012, <http://www.bts.gov/publications/national_transportation_statistics/html/table_01_11.html>; Gallup Poll, *Evolution, Creationism, Intelligent Design*, 2012, <http://www.gallup.com/poll/21814/evolution-creationism-intelligent-design.aspx>; Environmental Protection Agency, 2012, <http://www.epa.gov/epawaste/facts-text.htm#chart1>; Michael Marshall, 'Humanity weighs in at 287 million tonnes', 2012, <http://www.newscientist.com/article/dn21945-humanity-weighs-in-at-287-million-tonnes.html>

particularity still play an important role in creating unique cultural constellations. Arguing that cultural globalization always takes place in local contexts, Robertson rejects the cultural homogenization thesis and speaks instead of glocalization—a complex interaction of the global and local characterized by cultural borrowing. The resulting expressions of cultural 'hybridity' cannot be reduced to clear-cut manifestations of 'sameness' or 'difference'. As we noted in our discussion of Shakira and *Waka Waka* in Chapter 1, such processes of hybridization have become most visible in fashion, music, dance, film, food, and language.

But the respective arguments of hyperglobalizers and sceptics are not necessarily incompatible. The contemporary experience of living and acting across cultural borders means both the loss of traditional meanings and the creation of new symbolic expressions. Reconstructed feelings of belonging coexist in uneasy tension with a sense of placelessness. Indeed, some commentators have argued that modernity is slowly giving way to a new 'postmodern' framework characterized by a less stable sense of identity and knowledge.

Given the complexity of global cultural flows, one would actually expect to see uneven and contradictory effects. In certain contexts, these flows might change traditional manifestations of national identity in the direction of a popular culture characterized by sameness; in others they might foster new expressions of cultural particularism; in still others they might encourage forms of cultural 'hybridity'. Those commentators who summarily denounce the homogenizing effects of Americanization must not forget that hardly any society in the world today possesses an 'authentic', self-contained culture. Those who despair at the flourishing of cultural hybridity ought to listen to exciting Bollywood pop songs, admire the intricacy of several variations of Hawaiian pidgin, or enjoy the culinary delights of Cuban-Chinese cuisine. Finally, those who applaud the spread of consumerist

9. Jihad vs McWorld: selling fast food in Indonesia

capitalism need to pay attention to its negative consequences, such as the dramatic decline of traditional communal sentiments as well as the commodification of society and nature.

The role of the media

To a large extent, the global cultural flows of our time are generated and directed by global media empires that rely on powerful communication technologies to spread their message. Saturating global cultural reality with formulaic TV shows and mindless advertisements, these corporations increasingly shape people's identities and the structure of desires around the world. The rise of the global imaginary is inextricably connected to the rise of the global media. During the last two decades, a small group of very large TNCs have come to dominate the global market for entertainment, news, television, and film. In 2006, only eight media conglomerates—Yahoo, Google, AOL/Time Warner, Microsoft, Viacom, General Electric, Disney, and News Corporation—accounted for more than two-thirds of the US$250–275 billion in annual worldwide revenues generated by the communications industry. In the first half of that year, the volume of merger deals in global media, Internet, and telecommunications totalled US$300 billion, three times the figure for the first six months of 1999.

As recently as fifteen years ago, not one of the giant corporations that dominate what Benjamin Barber has appropriately called the 'infotainment telesector' existed in its present form as a media company. In 2001, nearly all of these corporations ranked among the largest 300 non-financial firms in the world. Today, most media analysts concede that the emergence of a global commercial-media market amounts to the creation of a global oligopoly similar to that of the oil and automotive industries in the early part of the 20th century. The crucial cultural innovators of earlier decades—small, independent record labels, radio stations, movie theatres, newspapers, and book publishers—have become virtually extinct as they found themselves incapable of competing with the media giants.

The commercial values disseminated by transnational media enterprises secure not only the undisputed cultural hegemony of popular culture, but also lead to the depoliticization of social reality and the weakening of civic bonds. One of the most glaring developments of the last two decades has been the transformation of news broadcasts and educational programmes into shallow entertainment shows—many of them ironically touted as 'reality' shows. Given that news is less than half as profitable as entertainment, media firms are increasingly tempted to pursue higher profits by ignoring journalism's much vaunted separation of newsroom practices and business decisions. Partnerships and alliances between news and entertainment companies are fast becoming the norm, making it more common for publishing executives to press journalists to cooperate with their newspapers' business operations. A sustained attack on the professional autonomy of journalism is, therefore, also part of cultural globalization.

The globalization of languages

One direct method of measuring and evaluating cultural changes brought about by globalization is to study the shifting global patterns of language use. The globalization of languages can be viewed as a process by which some languages are increasingly used in international communication while others lose their prominence and even disappear for lack of speakers. Researchers at the Globalization Research Center at the University of Hawai'i have identified five key variables that influence the globalization of languages:

1. *Number of languages*: The declining number of languages in different parts of the world points to the strengthening of homogenizing cultural forces.

2. *Movements of people*: People carry their languages with them when they migrate and travel. Migration patterns affect the spread of languages.
3. *Foreign language learning and tourism*: Foreign language learning and tourism facilitate the spread of languages beyond national or cultural boundaries.
4. *Internet languages*: The Internet has become a global medium for instant communication and quick access to information. Language use on the Internet is a key factor in the analysis of the dominance and variety of languages in international communication.
5. *International scientific publications*: International scientific publications contain the languages of global intellectual discourse, thus critically impacting intellectual communities involved in the production, reproduction, and circulation of knowledge around the world.

Given these highly complex interactions, research in this area frequently yields contradictory conclusions. The figure above represents only one possible conceptualization of the meaning and effects of language globalization. Unable to reach a general agreement, experts in the field have developed several different hypotheses. One model posits a clear correlation between the growing global significance of a few languages—particularly English, Chinese, and Spanish—and the declining number of other languages around the world. Another model suggests that the globalization of language does not necessarily mean that our descendants are destined to utilize only a few tongues. Still another thesis emphasizes the power of the Anglo-American culture industry to make English—or what some commentators call 'Globish'—*the* global lingua franca of the 21st century.

To be sure, the rising significance of the English language has a long history, reaching back to the birth of British colonialism in the late 16th century. At that time, only approximately seven

Continents	Early 16th Century (no./%)	Early 17th Century (no./%)	Early 18th Century (no./%)	Early 19th Century (no./%)	Early 20th Century (no./%)	Late 20th Century (no./%)
Americas	2,175/15	2,025/15	1,800/15	1,500/15	1,125/15	1,005/15
Africa	4,350/30	4,050/30	3,600/30	3,000/30	2,250/30	2,011/30
Europe	435/3	405/3	360/3	300/3	225/3	201/3
Asia	4,785/33	4,455/33	3,960/33	3,300/33	2,475/33	2,212/33
Pacific	2,755/19	2,565/19	2,280/19	1,900/19	1,425/19	1,274/19
World	14,500/100	13,500/100	12,000/100	10,000/100	7,500/100	6,703/100

H. The declining number of languages around the world, 1500–2000

Source: Globalization Research Center at the University of Hawai'i-Manoa

million people used English as their mother tongue. By the 1990s, this number had swollen to over 350 million native speakers, with 400 million more using English as a second language. Today, more than 80 per cent of the content posted on the Internet is in English. Almost half of the world's growing population of foreign students is enrolled at institutions in Anglo-American countries.

At the same time, however, the number of spoken languages in the world has dropped from about 14,500 in 1500 to less than 6,500 in 2012 (see Figure H). Given the current rate of decline, some linguists predict that 50–90 per cent of the currently existing languages will have disappeared by the end of the 21st century. But the world's languages are not the only entities threatened with extinction. The spread of consumerist values and materialist lifestyles has endangered the ecological health of our planet as well.

Chapter 6

The ecological dimension of globalization

Although we have examined the economic, political, and cultural aspects of globalization separately, it is important to emphasize that each of these dimensions impacts on and has consequences for the other domains. Nowhere is this more clearly demonstrated than in the ecological dimensions of globalization. In recent years, global environmental issues such as global climate change and transboundary pollution have received enormous attention from research institutes, the media, politicians, and economists. Indeed, the ecological effects of globalization are increasingly recognized as the most significant and potentially life threatening for the world as we have inherited it from our ancestors. The worldwide impact of natural and man-made disasters such as the horrifying nuclear plant accidents at Chernobyl, Ukraine (1986), and Fukushima, Japan (2011), clearly shows that the formidable ecological problems of our time can only be tackled by a global alliance of states and civil society actors.

In addition to economic and political factors, cultural values greatly influence how people view their natural environment. For example, cultures steeped in Taoist, Buddhist, and various animist religions tend to emphasize the interdependence of all living beings—a perspective that calls for a delicate balance between human wants and ecological needs. Judeo-Christian humanism, on the other hand, contains deeply dualistic values that put humans in control of nature. In Western modernity, the environment has thus come to be considered as a 'resource' to be used instrumentally to fulfil human needs and wants. The most extreme manifestation of this 'anthropocentric' paradigm is reflected in the dominant values and beliefs of consumerism. As pointed out previously, the capitalist culture industry seeks to convince its global audience that the meaning and chief value of life can be found in the limitless accumulation of material goods.

In the 21st century, however, it has become virtually impossible to ignore the fact that people everywhere on our planet are inextricably linked to each other through the air they breathe, the climate they depend upon, the food they eat, and the water they drink. In spite of this obvious lesson of interdependence, our planet's ecosystems are subjected to continuous human assault in order to maintain wasteful lifestyles. Granted, some of the major ecological challenges the world faces today are problems that afflicted civilizations even in ancient times. But until the coming of the Industrial Revolution, environmental degradation was relatively localized and occurred slowly over many centuries.

In the last few decades, however, the scale, speed, and depth of Earth's environmental decline have been unprecedented. Let us briefly consider some of the most dangerous manifestations of the globalization of environmental degradation.

Two major concerns relate to uncontrolled population growth and lavish consumption patterns in the global North. Since farming economies first came into existence about 480 generations ago, the global population has exploded a thousand-fold to reach seven billion in 2012. Half of this increase has occurred in the last thirty years. With the possible exception of some rodent species, humans are now the most numerous mammals on earth. Vastly increased demands for food, timber, and fibre have put severe pressure on the planet's ecosystems.

Large areas of the Earth's surface, especially in arid and semi-arid regions, have been used for agricultural production for millennia, yielding crops for ever-increasing numbers of people. Concerns about the relationship between population growth and environmental degradation are frequently focused rather narrowly on aggregate population levels. Yet, the global impact of humans on the environment is as much a function of per capita consumption as it is of overall population size (see Figure I). For example, the United States comprises only 6 per cent of the world's population, but it consumes 30–40 per cent of our planet's natural resources. Together, regional overconsumption and uncontrolled population growth present a serious problem to the health of our planet. Unless we are willing to change the underlying cultural and religious value structure that sustains these ominous dynamics, the health of Mother Earth is likely to deteriorate further.

Some of the effects of overconsumption and population growth are painfully obvious in the current food crisis plaguing vast regions of our planet. Large-scale food riots in Haiti, Indonesia, the Philippines, China, and Cameroon in the last few years highlight increasing limitations on access to food in part as a result of environmental problems such as drought. Other factors include rising oil prices (which affect the cost of transportation of food), diversion of food staples such as corn into production of biofuels in efforts to reduce reliance on oil, and unequal access to resources across developed and developing countries. The current food crisis highlights the interconnections between political, economic, and ecological problems that are accentuated by the process of globalization.

Another significant ecological problem associated with population increases and the globalization of environmental degradation is the worldwide reduction of biodiversity. Seven out of ten biologists today believe that the world is now in the midst of the fastest mass extinction of living species in the 4.5-billion-year history of the planet. According to recent Organisation for Economic Co-operation and Development (OECD) reports, two-thirds of the world's

	Annual oil consumption per capita (in litres)	Automobiles per 1000 people	Annual meat consumption per capita (in kg)	Annual withdrawal of fresh water per capita (in cubic metres)
USA	3,504	808	123	1,518
South Korea	2,606	379	54	525
Finland	2,397	591	73	436
Brazil	572	259	80	297
Egypt	513	43	22	809
Indonesia	302	79	11	356
DR Congo	10	5	5	5

I. Annual consumption patterns (per capita) in selected countries, 2010–12

Sources: Oil: *CIA World Factbook*, 2012, <https://www.cia.gov/library/publications/the-world-factbook/index.html>; Cars: World Bank, 2012, <http://data.worldbank.org/indicator/IS.VEH.NVEH.P3>; Meat: UN Food and Agriculture Organization, 2010, *Livestock and Fish Primary Equivalent*, <http://faostat.fao.org/site/291/default.aspx>; Water: Pacific Institute, *Worldwater.org*, <http://www.worldwater.org/images/pdf.gif>

farmlands have been rated as 'somewhat degraded' and one-third have been marked as 'strongly degraded'. Half the world's wetlands have already been destroyed, and the biodiversity of freshwater ecosystems is under serious threat. Three-quarters of worldwide genetic diversity in agricultural crop and animal breeds has been lost since 1900. Some experts fear that up to 50 per cent of all plant and animal species—most of them in the global South—will disappear by the end of this century. Hence, many environmentalists have argued that biodiversity should be treated as a planetary asset and held in trust for the benefit of future generations.

Some of the measures currently undertaken to safeguard biodiversity include the creation of hundreds of 'gene banks' located in over a hundred countries around the world. One of the most spectacular of these banks is the Svalbard Global Seed Vault buried in permafrost in a mountain on the Artic island of Spitzbergen. Officially opened in 2008, this 'Doomsday Vault' was funded by The Global Crop Diversity Trust (financed by international donors like the Gates and Rockefeller Foundations) and specially designed to store back-up copies of the seeds of the world's major food crops at minus 18 degrees Celsius. Operating like a safety deposit box in a bank, the Global Seed Vault is free of charge to public and private depositors and kept safe by the Norwegian government. But it is doubtful that such laudable 'back-up' measures are sufficient to reverse the escalating loss of biodiversity brought about by humanity's ecological footprint.

Transboundary pollution represents another grave danger to our collective survival. The release of vast amounts of synthetic chemicals into the air and water has created conditions for human and animal life that are outside previous limits of biological experience. For example, chlorofluorocarbons have been used in the second half of the 20th century as nonflammable refrigerants, industrial solvents, foaming agents, and aerosol propellants. In the mid-1970s, researchers noted that the unregulated release of CFCs into the air seemed to be depleting Earth's protective ozone layer. A decade later, the discovery of large 'ozone holes' over Tasmania, New Zealand, and large parts of the Antarctic finally resulted in a coordinated international effort to phase out production of CFCs and other ozone-depleting substances. In 2012, scientists warned that the risk of damage to the world's ozone layer has increased as a result of more frequent and severe storms as a result of global climate change. Other forms of transboundary pollution include industrial emissions of sulphur and nitrogen oxides. Returning to the ground in the form of 'acid rain', these chemicals damage forests, soils, and freshwater ecosystems. Current acid deposits in Northern Europe and parts of North America are at least twice as high as the critical level suggested by environmental agencies.

Finally, the issue of human-induced climate change has emerged as a major focus of domestic and intergovernmental policy as well as grass roots activism. Brought to public attention by former US Vice President Al Gore in the 2000s through his award-winning documentary, *An Inconvenient Truth*, as well as the production of numerous scientific reports outlining the dire consequences of unchecked global warming, climate change is clearly one of the top three 'global problems' facing humanity today. The consequences of worldwide climate change, especially global warming, could be catastrophic. A large number of scientists worldwide are calling for concerted action by governments to curb greenhouse gas emissions.

Indeed, global warming represents a grim example of the decisive shift in both the intensity and extent of contemporary environmental problems. The rapid build-up of gas emissions, including carbon dioxide, methane, nitrous and sulphur oxides, and chlorofluorocarbons in our planet's atmosphere has greatly enhanced Earth's capacity to trap heat. The resulting 'greenhouse effect' is responsible for raising average temperatures worldwide (see Illustration 10).

The precise effects of global warming are difficult to calculate. In 2006, Sir Nicholas Stern, former chief economist for the World

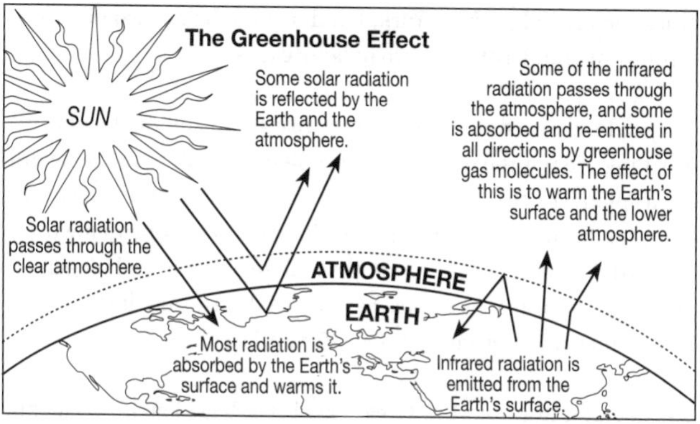

The Greenhouse Effect
SUN
Some solar radiation is reflected by the Earth and the atmosphere.
Some of the infrared radiation passes through the atmosphere, and some is absorbed and re-emitted in all directions by greenhouse gas molecules. The effect of this is to warm the Earth's surface and the lower atmosphere.
Solar radiation passes through the clear atmosphere.
ATMOSPHERE
EARTH
Most radiation is absorbed by the Earth's surface and warms it.
Infrared radiation is emitted from the Earth's surface.

10. The greenhouse effect

Bank, released a comprehensive and alarming report on the economic and ecological impacts of climate change. The 'Stern Report', commissioned by the UK government, asserts that average global temperatures have already risen by 0.5 degrees Celsius based on pre-industrialization temperatures. Based on current trends, average global temperatures will rise by an additional 2 to 3 degrees Celsius over the next fifty years. In the next century, they might rise another 3 degrees Celsius. In some parts of Africa, average temperatures have already risen by more than 3 degrees Celsius in the last twenty years.

These significant increases in global temperatures have been leading to meltdowns of large chunks of the world's major ice reserves. The North Polar ice cap, for example, has lost 15–20 per cent of its mass every decade since 1980 and might vanish by 2015. The complete melting of the large Greenland ice sheet would result in a global rise of sea levels of 22 feet. However, even a much smaller sea level rise would spell doom for many coastal regions around the world. The small Pacific island nations of Tuvalu and Kiribati, for example, would disappear. Large coastal cities such as Tokyo, New York, London, and Sydney would lose significant chunks of their urban landscapes.

But sea level and water temperature rise as a result of global warming are not the only serious problems threatening the health of our planet's oceans. Overfishing, the loss of coral reefs, coastal pollution, acidification, mega-oil spills such as the one following the 2010 BP oil rig explosion in the Gulf of Mexico, and illegal dumping of hazardous wastes have had a devastating impact on Earth's marine environments (see Figure J).

Consider, for example, the 'Great Pacific Garbage Patch'—a gigantic floating mass of often toxic, non-biodegradable plastics and chemical sludge twice the size of Texas that circulates permanently in the powerful currents of the Northern Pacific Ocean. Or, perhaps even more horrifying, take the huge floating debris field generated by the devastating Japanese earthquake and tsunami of March 2011 that killed more than 15,000 people across Japan. The disaster caused the partial destruction of the Fukushima Daiichi nuclear plant, in the process allowing the escape of harmful radioactive particles into air and water. Stretching for nearly 2,000 miles and still containing 1.5 million tons of detritus (3.5 million tons have already sunk), this debris field crossed the Pacific in only fifteen months. It deposited on North America's Pacific coast massive amounts of partially toxic materials such as wall insulation, oil and gas canisters, car tires, fishing nets, and Styrofoam buoys. Heavier items are drifting underwater and might wash up in years to come. Experts fear that some of these materials might exceed safe levels of radioactivity. Various computer models show that the debris field will circle back to Hawai'i, and possibly Japan, between 2013 and 2015, only to start anew its ominous journey toward the Pacific shores of North America.

The central feature of all these potentially disastrous environmental problems is that they are 'global', thus making them serious problems for all sentient beings inhabiting our

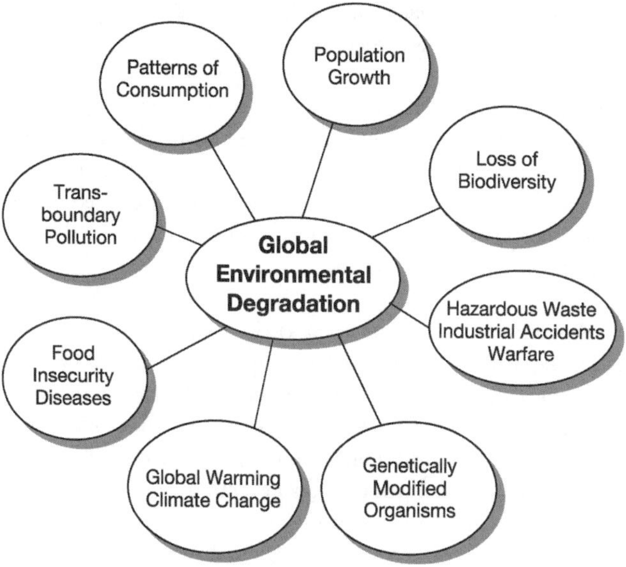

J. Major manifestations and consequences of global environmental degradation

Source: Author

magnificent blue planet. Indeed, transboundary pollution, global warming, climate change, and species extinction are challenges that cannot be contained within national or even regional borders. They do not have isolated causes and effects for they are caused by aggregate collective human actions and thus require a coordinated global response.

To be sure, ecological problems aggravated by globalization also have significant economic ramifications. Although these effects will be more significant for less developed countries than for rich countries, they will nonetheless affect all people and all nations. Poor countries do not have the necessary infrastructure or income to adapt to the unavoidable climate changes that will occur because of carbon emissions already in the earth's atmosphere. As we noted above, developing regions are already warmer on average than most developed countries and consequently suffer from a high degree of variability in rainfall. To make matters worse, less developed countries are also heavily dependent on agriculture for the majority of their income. Since agriculture is the most climate sensitive of all economic sectors, developing nations will be more adversely affected by climate change than developed countries.

Further consequences of this vicious circle include increased illnesses, escalating death rates, and crumbling infrastructure. The cost of living will continue to rise, leaving poor households and communities unable to save for future emergencies. Recent scientific reviews like the Stern Report explicitly link the problem of climate change to development and aid provision in poor countries. They will require assistance from the developed world if they are to adapt and survive climate change. Thus, climate change and global warming are not merely environmental or scientific issues. They are economic, political, cultural but above all ethical issues that have been expanded and intensified by the process of globalization.

There has been much debate in public and academic circles about the severity of climate change and the best ways for the global community to respond to it. As can be gleaned from the list of major global environmental treaties provided below, international discussion on the issue of global warming and environmental degradation has been occurring for over thirty years. Yet, while much has been written and spoken about this issue, few coordinated measures have been implemented. Most international environmental treaties still lack effective enforcement mechanisms.

For the most part, political will in favour of immediate change has been weak and limited. However, the most significant obstacles to the creation and implementation of an effective global environmental agreement has come from the unwillingness of China and the United States—the world's two largest polluters—to ratify key agreements. Both nations see measures to reduce carbon emissions and thereby slow global warming as threats to their economic growth. Yet inaction on climate change today will have more dire consequences for economic growth tomorrow. (see Figures K and L).

Still, there are some grounds for guarded optimism. For example, significant agreement exists that certain limitations on carbon emissions must be placed on all nations. Some rich countries in the EU and Australia managed to impose a national carbon tax on emitters. But poor countries argue that they should not be bound by the same carbon measures or trading schemes as developed countries. They make this argument for two reasons. Firstly, they need to build up their industries and infrastructures in order to pull themselves out of poverty. Placing significant carbon emissions restrictions on their industries would seriously impede their economic development. Secondly, they argue that poor countries have not been responsible for the production of most of the greenhouse gases that have caused the current problem. Identifying developed countries as the primary producers of greenhouse gases, they suggest that the major burden for limiting the production of greenhouse gases should fall on the developed world—at least until developing countries have pulled their populations out of extreme poverty.

The United States has expressed strong opposition to these arguments by insisting that all countries should be subjected to the same limitations on carbon emissions. At the Thirteenth Conference of the Parties (COP 13) to the United Nations Framework Convention on Climate Change (UNFCCC) in Bali 2007, the US delegation repeatedly blocked negotiations by demanding that developing countries take more responsibility for their contribution to global warming. At the same time,

Country	Total emissions (1000 tons of CO_2)	Per capita emissions (tonnes/capita)	Per capita emissions (rank)
China (mainland)	1,917,621	5.3	78
United States of America	1,546,903	17.5	12
India	475,238	1.4	145
Russian Federation	465,954	12.1	23
Japan	329,469	9.5	38
Germany	214,524	9.6	37
Canada	148,375	16.4	15
Islamic Republic of Iran	146,824	7.3	54
United Kingdom	142,584	5.3	43
Republic of Korea	138,852	10.6	28
Mexico	129,761	4.4	90
Italy	121,385	7.5	52
South Africa	118,865	8.8	42
Saudi Arabia	118,232	17.2	13
Indonesia	110,725	1.8	130
Australia	108,868	18.9	11
Brazil	107,232	1.9	124
France	102,805	6.1	65
Spain	89,797	7.4	53
Ukraine	88,228	7.0	57
Global Average	–	1.3	–

K. The top 20 carbon dioxide emitters, 2008–10

Sources: CDIAC, *Top 20 Emitting Countries by Total Fossil-Fuel CO_2 Emissions for 2008*, <http://cdiac.ornl.gov/trends/emis/tre_tp20.html>; UN, Per capita estimates, <http://data.un.org/Data.aspx?d=MDG&f=seriesRowID%3a751>

however, America has been reluctant to enter into any agreement that might slow its own economic growth. Throughout the 2000s, the Bush administration walked away from key international treaties such as the Kyoto Protocol

Year	Million metric tonnes of carbon
1750	3
1800	8
1850	54
1900	534
1950	1,630
2000	6,750
2008	8,749

L. Long term global CO_2 emissions

Source: CDIAC, 2011, <http://cdiac.ornl.gov/ftp/ndp030/global.1751_2008.ems>

while remaining significantly behind other developed countries in its commitments on capping and reducing carbon emissions.

Unfortunately, the next US government did not fundamentally break with the approach of its predecessor. Although President Barack Obama made stronger rhetorical gestures in favour of environmental protection, his actions did not match his words. For example, at the 2009 Copenhagen Climate Summit, Obama acquiesced to unspecific, non-legally binding agreements that fell far short of the Summit's goal to establish a strong and binding global climate agreement by 2012.

In the same vein, the much anticipated 2012 UN conference on Sustainable Development in Brazil—known as Rio + 20 because it was held twenty years after the historic 1992 Rio Summit on Climate Change—merely produced toothless documents that paid lip service to a 'common vision' of environmental sustainability but failed to mandate binding emission reduction targets. National states proved themselves to be unwilling to engage in the sort of environmental multilateralism that would produce measurable results in the worldwide struggle against global warming. The only major achievement of Rio + 20 was the launching of the 'People's Sustainability Manifesto' by hundreds of civil society organizations which seek to build a global-local movement for the protection of the environment. The next UN Climate Summit to be held in Qatar in 2013—the country with the world's highest per capita carbon emissions—is unlikely to break the pattern of weak and non-binding state action (see Figure M).

In their comprehensive study, *Globalization and the Environment* (2013), the Australian political scientists Peter Christoff and Robyn Eckersley have identified five deep-seated and interlocking problems that have prevented the creation and ratification of an effective global environmental treaty system:

1. States have failed to integrate environmental and economic governance at the national level.
2. States have failed to integrate environmental and economic governance at the international level.
3. Powerful social forces continue to resist or co-opt efforts to transform economies and societies in a more ecologically sustainable direction.
4. The neoliberal economic discourse remains globally dominant, undermining sustainable development and ecological modernization discourses and practices.
5. All of the above persists because national and international accountability mechanisms remain weak and inadequate in a globalizing world.

Many leading scientists believe that a further decade of inaction would make it impossible to avoid the disastrous impacts of climate change and ecological degradation. Indeed, the 2012 edition of the UN Environment Program's *Global Environmental Outlook* confirms their worst fears by documenting a planet

Name of Treaty/Conference	Coverage/protection	Date
Ramsar Convention	Iran wetlands	1971
UNESCO-World Heritage, Paris	Cultural and natural heritage	1972
UNEP Conference, Stockholm	General environment	1972
CITES, Washington, D.C.	Endangered species	1973
Marine pollution treaty, London	Marine pollution from ships	1978
UN Convention on Law of the Sea	Marine species, pollution	1982
Vienna Protocol	Ozone layer	1985
Montreal Protocol	Ozone layer	1987
Basel Convention	Hazardous wastes	1989
UN 'Rio Summit' on Environmental Climate Change	Biodiversity	1992
Jakarta Mandate	Marine and coastal diversity	1995
Kyoto Protocol	Global warming	1997
Rotterdam Convention	Industrial pollution	1998
Johannesburg World Summit	Ecological sustainability, pollution	2002
Bali Action Plan	Global warming	2007
UN Copenhagen Climate Summit	Global warming	2009
UN Cancun Climate Summit	Global warming	2010
UN Durban Climate Summit	Global warming	2011
UN Rio + 20	Sustainable development	2012

M. Major global environmental treaties/conferences, 1971–2012

Source: Author

pushed to its ecological limits. Confronted with the ill health of our Mother Earth in the second decade of the 21st century, it has become abundantly clear to many people that the contemporary phase of globalization has been the most environmentally destructive period of human history. It remains to be seen, however, whether the growing recognition of the ecological limits of our planet will translate into tackling the five problems identified above by Christoff and Eckersley. As they note in Point 4, much depends on counteracting powerful ideologies that are rooted in the worship of unfettered markets and the desire for the unlimited accumulation and consumption of material things.

Chapter 7
Ideologies of globalization: market globalism, justice globalism, religious globalisms

Ideologies are powerful systems of widely shared ideas and patterned beliefs that are accepted as truth by significant groups in society. Serving as political mental maps, they offer people a more or less coherent picture of the world not only as it is, but also as it ought to be. In doing so, ideologies help organize the tremendous complexity of the human experiences into fairly simple claims that serve as guide and compass for social and political action.

These claims are employed to legitimize certain political interests and to defend or challenge dominant power structures. Seeking to imbue society with their preferred norms and values, the codifiers of ideologies—usually social elites—provide the public with a circumscribed agenda of things to discuss, claims to make, and questions to ask. These power elites speak to their audience in narratives that persuade, praise, condemn, distinguish 'truths' from 'falsehoods', and separate the 'good' from the 'bad'. Thus, ideology connects theory and practice by orienting and organizing human action in accordance with generalized claims and codes of conduct.

Like all social processes, globalization operates on an ideological dimension filled with a range of norms, claims, beliefs, and narratives about the phenomenon itself. Indeed, the heated public debate over whether globalization represents a 'good' or a 'bad' thing occurs in the arena of ideology. But before we explore the ideological dimension of globalization in more detail, we should recall our important analytical distinction between *globalization*—a set of social processes of intensifying global interdependence—and *globalisms*—ideologies that endow the concept of globalization with particular values and meanings.

Today, three types of globalism compete for adherents around the globe. *Market globalism* seeks to endow 'globalization' with free-market norms and neoliberal meanings. Contesting market globalism from the political Left, *justice globalism* constructs an alternative vision of globalization based on egalitarian ideals of global solidarity and distributive justice. From the political Right, various *religious globalisms* struggle against both market globalism and justice globalism as they seek to mobilize a religious community imagined in global terms in defence of religious values and beliefs that are thought to be under severe attack by the forces of secularism and consumerism.

In spite of their considerable differences, however, these three globalisms share nonetheless an important function: they articulate and translate the rising global imaginary—a background understanding of community and belonging increasingly tied to the global—into concrete political programs and agendas. Hence, it would be inaccurate to accuse the two ideological challengers of dominant market globalism of being 'anti-globalization'. Rather, their position could be described as 'alter-globalization'—subscribing to alternative visions of an integrated world that resist neoliberal projections of universal free-market principles.

To be sure, there are powerful voices of 'anti-globalization'—national-populists and economic protectionists such as Patrick Buchanan and many Tea Party adherents in the United States, Marine Le Pen in France, Nick Griffin in the UK, or Karl-Heinz Strache in Austria. Their respective programs look very similar in their fierce opposition to globalizing dynamics that challenge national unity imagined in homogenous terms. Buchanan, for example, supports in his best-selling books and fiery political speeches 'economic nationalism'—the view that the economy should be designed in ways that serve narrow national interests. He frequently expresses the conviction that there exists at the core of contemporary American society an irrepressible conflict between the claims of American nationalism and the commands of the global economy. In Buchanan's opinion, most mainstream American politicians are beholden to transnational corporate interests that are undermining the sovereignty of the nation by supporting a global governance structure headed by the World Trade Organization (WTO) and other international institutions. He also accuses 'globalist advocates of multiculturalism' of opening the doors to millions of immigrants who are allegedly responsible for the economic and moral decline of the United States.

Five rhetorical manoeuvres performed by national-populists

1. The emotional construction of unbridgeable political differences dividing the population into the majority of 'good' ordinary people ('us') and a small but powerful and 'bad' elite ('them');
2. Frequent verbal attacks of the people's 'enemies' from a moralistic high-ground rather than a political level playing field;
3. The evocation of an extreme crisis brought on by the enemies of the people which requires an immediate and forceful response;
4. The imagination of the people as a homogenous national unit welded together by a common will and interests, an ancestral heartland, and shared cultural and religious traditions;
5. The rejection of globalization and multiculturalism as ominous dynamics threatening to destroy the national community.

Fearing the loss of national self-determination and the destruction of their national cultures, anti-globalization voices like Buchanan pledge to protect their nation from those 'foreign elements' they consider responsible for unleashing the forces of globalization. Clinging to the weakening national imaginary, national-populists regard autonomous nation-states as the only legitimate form of community. Hence, they can be viewed as 'reactionaries' in the sense of reacting against all three globalist ideologies without providing their national audiences with constructive articulations of the rising global imaginary.

Market globalism

Market globalism is without question the dominant ideology of our time. Since the 1990s, it has been codified and disseminated worldwide by global power elites that include corporate managers, executives of large transnational corporations, corporate lobbyists, influential journalists and public-relations specialists, intellectuals writing for a large public audience, celebrities and top entertainers, state bureaucrats, and politicians. (see Illustration 11).

Serving as the chief advocates of market globalism, these individuals saturate the public discourse with idealized images of a consumerist, free-market world. Selling their preferred version of a single global marketplace to the public, they portray globalization in a positive light as an indispensable tool for the realization of such a global order. Such favourable visions of globalization pervade public opinion and political choices in many parts of the world. Indeed, neoliberal decision-makers emerged as expert designers of an attractive ideological container for their market-friendly political agenda. Given that the exchange of commodities constitutes the core activity of all societies, the market-oriented discourse of globalization itself has turned into an extremely important commodity destined for public

11. Microsoft CEO, Bill Gates, one of the world's most powerful advocates of market globalism

consumption. *Business Week*, *The Economist*, *Forbes*, the *Wall Street Journal*, and the *Financial Times* are among the most powerful of dozens of magazines, journals, newspapers, and electronic media published globally that feed their readers a steady diet of market-globalist claims.

Thus, market globalism has become what some social theorists call a 'strong discourse'—one that is notoriously difficult to resist and repel because it has on its side powerful social forces that have already pre-selected what counts as 'real' and, therefore, shape the world accordingly. The constant repetition and public recitation of market globalism's core claims and slogans have the capacity to produce what they name. As more neoliberal policies are enacted, the claims of market globalism become even more firmly planted in the public mind.

Analysing hundreds of newspaper and magazine articles—both online and offline—I have identified five major ideological claims that occur with great regularity in the utterances, speeches, and writings of influential market globalists.

The five claims of market globalism

1. Globalization is about the liberalization and global integration of markets
2. Globalization is inevitable and irreversible
3. Nobody is in charge of globalization
4. Globalization benefits everyone
5. Globalization furthers the spread of democracy in the world

It is important to note that globalists themselves construct these ideological claims in order to sell their political and economic agenda. Perhaps no single market-globalist speech or piece of writing contains all of the five assertions discussed below, but all of them contain at least some of these claims.

Like all ideologies, market globalism starts with the attempt to establish an authoritative definition of its core concepts. For neoliberals, such an account is anchored in the idea of the self-regulating market that serves as the framework for a future global order. As we noted in Chapter 3, neoliberals seek to cultivate in the public discourse the uncritical association of 'globalization' with what they assert to be the benefits of market liberalization. In particular, they present the liberalization and integration of global markets as 'natural' phenomena that further individual liberty and material progress in the world. Here are two examples of claim 1:

> Globalization is about the triumph of markets over governments. Both proponents and opponents of Globalization agree that the driving force today is markets, which are suborning the role of government.
>
> *Business Week*, 13 December 1999

> One role [of government] is to get out of the way—to remove barriers to the free flow of goods, services, and capital.
>
> Joan Spero, former US Under-Secretary of State in the Clinton administration

The problem with claim 1 is that its core message of liberalizing and integrating markets is only realizable through the *political* project of engineering free markets. Thus, market globalists must be prepared to utilize the *powers of government* to weaken and eliminate those social policies and institutions that curtail the market. Since only strong governments are up to this ambitious task of transforming existing social arrangements, the successful liberalization of markets depends upon *intervention* and *interference* by centralized state power. Such actions, however, stand in stark contrast to the neoliberal idealization of the limited role of government. Yet, globalists do expect governments to play an extremely active role in implementing their political agenda. The activist character of the earliest neoliberal administrations in the United States, the United Kingdom, Australia, and New Zealand during the 1980s and 1990s attests to the importance of strong governmental action in engineering free markets.

Moreover, the claim that globalization is about the liberalization and global integration of markets solidifies as 'fact' what is actually a contingent political initiative. Market globalists have been successful because they have persuaded the public that their neoliberal account of globalization represents an objective, or at least a neutral, diagnosis of the very conditions it purports to analyse. To be sure, neoliberals may indeed be able to offer some 'empirical evidence' for the 'liberalization' of markets. But does the spread of market principles really happen because there exists a metaphysical connection between globalization and the expansion of markets? More likely, it occurs because globalists have the political and discursive power to shape the world largely according to their ideological formula:

LIBERALIZATION + INTEGRATION OF MARKETS
= GLOBALIZATION.

Claim 2 establishes the historical inevitability and irreversibility of globalization understood as the liberalization and global integration of markets. Let us consider the following statements:

> Today we must embrace the inexorable logic of globalization—that everything from the strength of our economy to the safety of our cities, to the health of our people, depends on events not only within our borders, but half a world away... Globalization is irreversible.
>
> Bill Clinton, former US President

> We need much more liberalization and deregulation of the Indian economy. No sensible Indian businessman disagrees with this... Globalization is inevitable. There is no better alternative.
>
> Rahul Bajaj, Indian industrialist

The portrayal of globalization as some sort of natural force, like the weather or gravity, makes it easier for market globalists to convince people that they must adapt to the discipline of the market if they are to survive and prosper. Hence, the claim of inevitability depoliticizes the public discourse about globalization. Neoliberal policies are portrayed to be above politics; they simply carry out what is ordained by nature. This implies that, instead of acting according to a set of choices, people merely fulfil world-market laws that demand the elimination of government controls. As former British Prime Minister Margaret Thatcher used to say, 'There is no alternative'. If nothing can be done about the natural movement of economic and technological forces, then political groups ought to acquiesce and make the best of an unalterable situation. Resistance would be unnatural, irrational, and dangerous.

Market globalism's deterministic language offers yet another rhetorical advantage. If the natural laws of the market have indeed preordained a neoliberal course of history, then globalization does not reflect the arbitrary agenda of a particular social class or group. In that case, market globalists merely carry out the unalterable imperatives of a transcendental force. People aren't in charge of globalization; markets and technology are. Here are two examples of claim 3:

> And the most basic truth about globalization is this: *No one is in charge*... We all want to believe that someone is in charge and responsible. But the global marketplace today is an Electronic Herd of often anonymous stock, bond and currency traders and multinational investors, connected by screens and networks.
>
> Thomas Friedman, *New York Times* correspondent and award-winning author

> The great beauty of globalization is that no one is in control. The great beauty of globalization is that it is not controlled by any individual, any government, any institution.
>
> Robert Hormats, former Vice Chairman of Goldman Sachs International

But Mr Hormats is right only in a formal sense. While there is no conscious conspiracy orchestrated by a single, evil force, this does not mean that nobody is in charge of globalization. The liberalization and integration of global markets does not proceed outside the realm of human choice. As we will discuss in the final chapter, the market-globalist initiative to integrate and deregulate markets around the world both creates and sustains asymmetrical power relations. Despite the rise of China, the United States is still the strongest economic and military power in the world, and the largest transnations corporations (TNCs) are based in North America. This is not to say that the 'American Empire' rules supremely over these gigantic processes of globalization. But it *does* suggest that both the substance and the direction of globalization are to a significant degree shaped by American domestic and foreign policy.

Claim 4—globalization benefits everyone—lies at the very core of market globalism because it provides an affirmative answer to the crucial normative question of whether globalization should be considered a 'good' or a 'bad' thing. Market globalists frequently connect their arguments to the alleged benefits resulting from trade liberalization: rising global living standards, economic efficiency, individual freedom, and unprecedented technological progress. Let us consider the following two examples:

> There can be little doubt that the extraordinary changes in global finance on balance have been beneficial in facilitating significant improvements in economic structures and living standards throughout the world....
>
> Alan Greenspan, former Chairman of the US Federal Reserve Board

> Globalization's effects have been overwhelmingly good. Spurred by unprecedented liberalization, world trade continues to expand faster than overall global economic output, inducing a wave of productivity and efficiency and creating millions of jobs.
>
> Peter Sutherland, former Chairman of British Petroleum

Mr Sutherland does not seem to question the ideological assumptions behind his statement. Where are 'millions of jobs' created? Who has benefited from globalization? As we discussed in Chapter 3, when the market goes too far in dominating social and political outcomes, the opportunities and rewards of globalization are spread often unequally, concentrating power and wealth amongst a select group of people, regions, and corporations at the expense of the multitude.

China and India are often referred to as the great 'winners' of globalization. But their astonishing economic growth and the rise of per capita income comes disproportionately from the top 10 per cent of the population. Indeed, the incomes of the

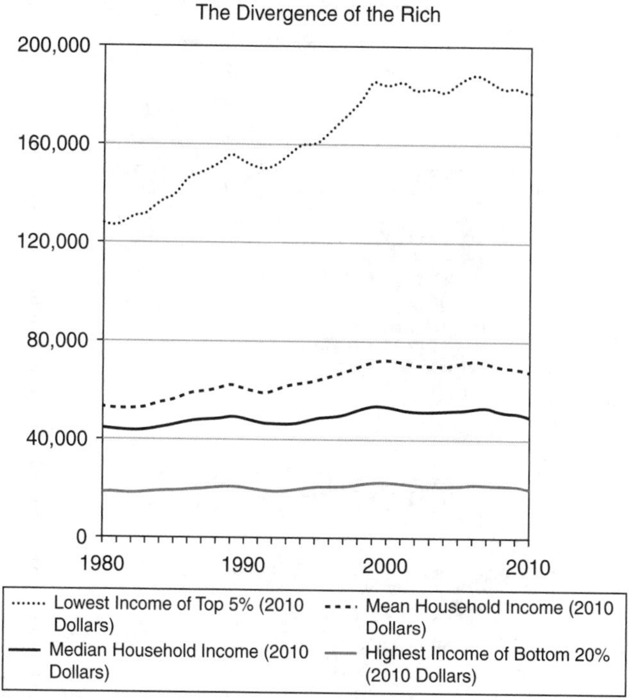

N. Income divergence in the USA, 1980–2010

Source: <www.census.gov/hhes/www/income/data/historical/household/index.html>

bottom 50 per cent in India and China have actually stagnated or even declined during the 2000s. Empirical evidence suggests that income disparities within and between nations are widening at a quicker pace than ever before in recent history.

Data published in the 1999 and 2000 editions of the *UN Human Development Report* show that, before the onset of globalization in 1973, the income ratio between the richest and poorest countries was at about 44 to 1. Twenty-five years later it had climbed to 74 to

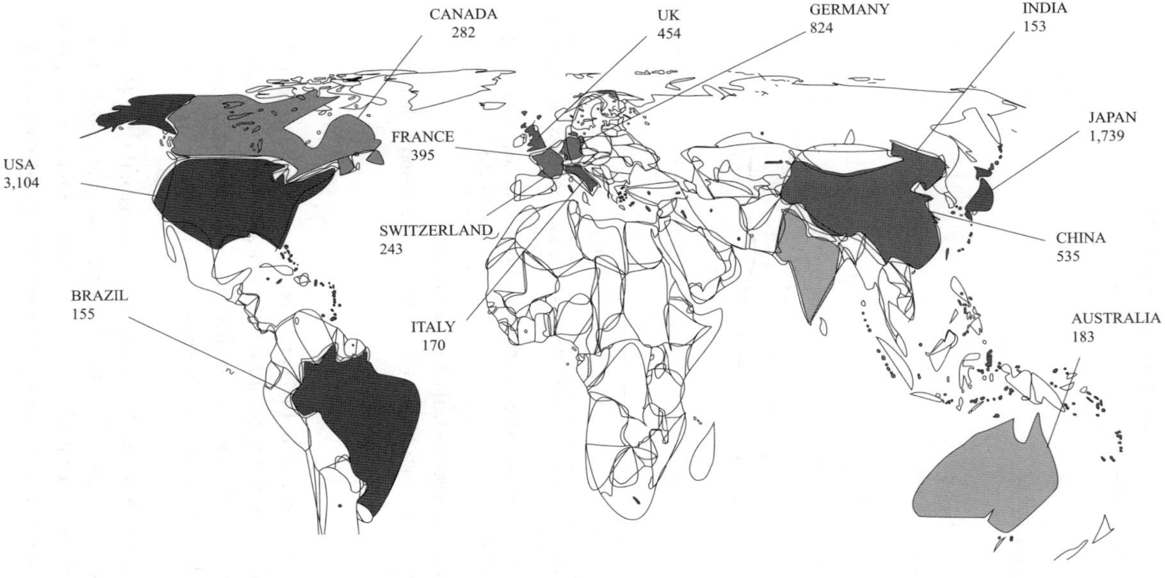

Map 5. Geography of the rich: number of people in thousands with investable assets of $1 million or more (2010)

Source: <http://www.tni.org> (data from the 2011 World Wealth Report)

1. In spite of some progress in alleviating poverty worldwide, the bottom 25 per cent of humankind in 2012 lived on less than $140 a year. Meanwhile, the assets of the world's top *three* billionaires are more than the combined GNP of all the least developed countries and their 600 million people.

There are numerous other indications confirming that the global hunt for profits actually makes it more difficult for poor people to enjoy the benefits of technology and scientific innovation. For example, there is widespread evidence for the existence of a widening 'digital divide' separating countries in the global North and South (see Figure O).

Claim 5—globalization furthers the spread of democracy in the world—is rooted in the neoliberal assertion that free markets and democracy are synonymous terms. Persistently affirmed as 'common sense', the actual compatibility of these concepts often goes unchallenged in the public discourse. Here are two examples:

> The level of economic development resulting from globalization is conducive to the creation of complex civil societies with a powerful middle class. It is this class and societal structure that facilitates democracy.
>
> Francis Fukuyama, Stanford University

> The Electronic Herd will intensify pressures for democratization generally, for three very critical reasons—flexibility, legitimacy, and sustainability.
>
> Thomas Friedman, *New York Times* correspondent and bestselling author

These arguments hinge on a conception of democracy that emphasizes formal procedures such as voting at the expense of the direct participation of broad majorities in political and economic decision-making. This 'thin' definition of democracy reflects an elitist and regimented model of 'low-intensity' or 'formal' market democracy. In practice, the crafting of a few democratic elements

World Regions	Population (2011 est.)	Population % of World	Internet Users, Latest Data 2012	% Population (Penetration)	Usage % World	% Usage Growth 2000-2011
Africa	1,037,524,058	15.0	139,875,242	13.5	6.2	2,988.4
Asia	3,876,740,877	56.0	1,016,799,076	26.2	44.8	789.6
Europe	816,426,346	11.8	500,723,686	61.3	22.1	376.4
Middle East	216,258,843	3.1	77,020,995	35.6	3.4	2,224.8
North America	347,394,870	5.0	273,067,546	78.6	12.0	152.6
Latin America/Caribbean	597,283,165	8.6	235,819,740	39.5	10.4	1,205.1
Oceania/Australia	35,426,995	0.5	23,927,457	67.5	1.1	241.0
World Total	6,930,055,154	100	2,267,233,742	32.7	100	528.1

O. Global Internet users as a percentage of the regional population

Source: <www.census.gov/hhes/www/income/data/historical/household/index.html>

onto a basically authoritarian structure ensures that those elected remain insulated from popular pressures and thus can govern 'effectively'. Hence, the assertion that globalization furthers the spread of democracy in the world is largely based on a superficial definition of democracy.

Our examination of the five central claims of market globalism suggests that the neoliberal language about globalization is ideological in the sense that it is politically motivated and contributes toward the construction of particular meanings of globalization that preserve and stabilize existing power relations. But the ideological reach of market globalism goes far beyond the task of providing the public with a narrow explanation of the meaning of globalization. Market globalism consists of powerful narratives that sell an overarching neoliberal worldview, thereby creating collective meanings and shaping people's identities. Yet, as both massive justice-globalist protests and jihadist-globalist acts of terrorism have shown, the expansion of market globalism has encountered considerable resistance from both the political Left and Right.

Justice globalism

As the 20th century was drawing to a close, criticisms of market globalism began to receive more attention in the public discourse on globalization, a development aided by a heightened awareness of how extreme corporate profit strategies were leading to widening global disparities in wealth and well-being. Starting in the late 1990s and continuing throughout much of the 2000s, the contest between market globalism and its ideological challenger on the political Left erupted in street confrontations in many cities around the world. Who are these justice-globalist forces and what is their ideological vision?

Justice globalism refers to the political ideas and values associated with the social alliances and political actors increasingly known as the 'social justice movement'. It emerged in the 1990s as a progressive network of non-governmental organizations (NGOs) that see themselves as a 'global civil society' dedicated to the establishment of a more equitable relationship between the global North and South, the protection of the global environment, fair trade and international labour issues, human rights, and women's issues.

Challenging the central claims of market globalism discussed in the previous chapter, justice globalists believe that 'another world is possible', as one of their central slogans suggests. Envisioning the construction of a new world order based on a global redistribution of wealth and power, justice globalists emphasize the crucial connection between globalization and local well-being. They accuse market-globalist elites of pushing neoliberal policies that are leading to greater global inequality, high levels of unemployment, environmental degradation, and the demise of social welfare. Calling for a 'Global New Deal' favouring the marginalized and poor, justice globalists seek to protect ordinary people all over the world from a neoliberal 'globalization from above'.

In the United States, the consumer advocate, Ralph Nader, and the human rights proponent, Noam Chomsky, are leading representatives of justice globalism. In Europe, the spokespersons for established Green parties have long suggested that unfettered neoliberal globalization has resulted in a serious degradation of the global environment. Neo-anarchist groups in Europe and the United States such as the 'Black Bloc' concur with this perspective, and some of these groups are willing to make selective use of violent means in order to achieve their objectives. In the global South, justice globalism is often represented by democratic-popular movements of resistance against neoliberal policies. Most of these groups have forged close links to other justice-globalist international non-governmental organizations INGOs.

Name of Organization	*Location*	*Areas of Concern/Focus*
Association pour une taxation des transactions financières pour l'aide aux citoyens (Association for the Taxation of Financial Transactions for the Aid of Citizens (ATTAC))	Paris, France plus multiple regional offices	Reform of global financial institutions and infrastructure
Articulacion Feminista Mercosur (Southern Common Market)	Montevideo, Uruguay	Rights of women, indigenous people, and the marginalized
Africa Trade Network	East Legon, Accra, Ghana	Trade and investment issues in Africa; reform of global financial system
Corpwatch	San Francisco, California, USA	Human, environmental, and worker rights at the local, national, and global levels; transparency and accountability into global finance and trade
Food First International Action Network	Heidelberg, Germany	Promote the right to food, food sovereignty, and food security around the world
Focus on the Global South	Manila, Philippines; Bangkok, Thailand; Delhi, India	Policy research, advocacy, activism, and grassroots capacity building; critique of corporate-led globalization, neo-liberalism, and militarization
International Forum on Globalization	San Francisco, USA	Think tank providing critique of neoliberal globalization; emphasizes developing alternate global trade and commerce that promotes interests of people and environment
Instituto Paulo Freire	Sao Paulo, Brazil	Right to education globally
Jubilee South	Manila, Philippines	Debt cancellation, reform of global financial rules and institutions, redistribution of wealth and resources
OneWorld Foundation	London, UK	Information organization; facilitate networks amongst organizations committed to justice, equality, democracy, action on climate change, poverty, development, and resource distribution
Terre des Hommes	Brussels, Belgium and Geneva, Switzerland	Focus on the rights of children globally
Transnational Institute	Amsterdam, The Netherlands	Network of activist-scholars promoting democracy, equality, and environmental sustainability on a global scale

P. Examples of justice-globalist organizations

Source: Author

Today, there exist thousands of these organizations in all parts of the world. Some consist only of a handful of activists, while others attract a much larger membership (see Figure P).

In the early 21st century, the forces of justice globalism have gathered political strength. This is evidenced by the emergence of the World Social Forum (WSF) and various 'Occupy' movements around the world. In the US, Occupy Wall Street burst onto the political scene in 2011 as part of a global Occupy movement that drew activists in the world's major cities within months. Inspired by the popular protests of the 'Arab Spring' and *Los Indignados* ('the indigents') encampments in Spain, Occupy demonstrators expressed outrage at the inequalities of global capitalism and the irresponsible practices of many financial institutions, all of which had been on stark display during the Global Financial Crisis. Brandishing their slogan 'We are the 99 per cent', Occupy protesters across the world occupied spaces of symbolic importance—such as New York City's Zuccotti Park near Wall Street—and sought to create—in miniature—the kind of egalitarian society they wanted to live in. Rejecting conventional organizational leadership formations, Occupy formed General Assemblies and working groups that reached decisions through a consensus-based process.

In spite of the mass appeal of the Occupy movement, however, the WSF still serves as the key ideological site of justice globalism. It draws to its annual meetings in Brazil or India tens of thousands of delegates from around the world. The proponents of justice globalism deliberately set up the WSF as a 'shadow organization' to the market-globalist World Economic Forum (WEF) in Davos, Switzerland. Just like market globalists who treat the WEF as a platform to project their ideas and values to a global audience, justice globalists utilize the WSF as the main production site of their ideological and policy alternatives.

From the WSF Charter of Principles

1. The World Social Forum is an open meeting place for reflective thinking, democratic debate of ideas, formulation of proposals, free exchange of experiences, and interlinking for effective action by groups and movements of civil society that are opposed to neoliberalism and to domination of the world by capital and any form of imperialism and are committed to building a planetary society directed toward fruitful relationships among humankind and between it and the Earth....

8. The World Social Forum is a plural, diversified, confessional, nongovernmental, and non-party context that, in a decentralized fashion, interrelates organizations and movements engaged in concrete action at levels from the local to the international to build another world....

13. As a context for interrelations, the World Social Forum seeks to strengthen and create new national and international links among organizations and movement of society that—in both public and private life—will increase the capacity for non-violent social resistance to the process of dehumanization the world is undergoing....

Most of the justice-globalist groups affiliated with the WSF started out as small, seemingly insignificant groups of like-minded people in South America and Europe. Many of them learned important theoretical and practical lessons from justice-globalist struggles in developing countries, particularly from Mexico's Zapatista rebellion.

On 1 January 1994, the day NAFTA went into effect, a small band of indigenous rebels calling themselves the *Zapatista Army of National Liberation* captured four cities in the Chiapas region of southeast Mexico. Engaging in a number of skirmishes with the

Five principal claims of justice globalism

1. Neoliberalism produces global crises.
2. Market-driven globalization has increased worldwide disparities in wealth and wellbeing.
3. Democratic participation is essential in solving global problems.
4. Another world is possible and urgently needed.
5. People power, not corporate power!

Mexican army and police over the next few years, the Zapatistas continued to protest the implementation of NAFTA and what their leader, Subcomandante Marcos, called the 'global economic process to eliminate that multitude of people who are not useful to the powerful'. In addition, the Zapatistas put forward a comprehensive programme that pledged to reverse the destructive consequences of neoliberal free-market policies. Although the Zapatistas insisted that a major part of their struggle related to the restoration of the political and economic rights of indigenous peoples and the poor in Mexico, they also emphasized that the fight against neoliberalism had to be waged globally.

The legendary 'Battle of Seattle' in late 1999 was the first in a decade-long series of large-scale confrontations between the forces of market globalism and justice globalism. 40,000 to 50,000 people took part in this massive anti-WTO protest in Seattle, Washington. In spite of the predominance of North American participants, there was also a significant international presence. Activists like José Bové, a French sheep farmer who became an international celebrity for trashing a McDonald's outlet, marched shoulder to shoulder with Indian farmers and leaders of the Philippines' peasant movement. Articulating some of the five principal justice-globalist claims featured above, this eclectic alliance included consumer activists, labour activists (including students demonstrating against sweatshops), environmentalists, animal rights activists, advocates of Third World debt relief, feminists, and human rights proponents. Criticizing the WTO's neoliberal position on agriculture, multilateral investments, and intellectual property rights, this impressive crowd represented more than 700 organizations and groups.

Eventually, large groups of demonstrators interrupted traffic in the city centre and managed to block off the main entrances to the convention centre by forming human chains. As hundreds of delegates were scrambling to make their way to the conference centre, Seattle police employed tear gas, batons, rubber bullets, and pepper spray stingers against the demonstrators (see Illustration 12). Altogether, the police arrested over 600 persons.

12. Police use tear gas to push back WTO protesters in downtown Seattle, 30 November 1999

Ironically, the Battle of Seattle proved that many of the new technologies hailed by market globalists as the true hallmark of globalization could also be employed in the service of justice-globalist forces and their political agenda. Text-messaging on mobile devices enabled the organizers of events like the one in Seattle to arrange for new forms of protest such as a series of demonstrations held simultaneously in various cities around the globe. As we have seen in the 2011 revolutions in the Middle East and the Occupy protests around the world, individuals and groups all over the world can utilize applications like Twitter and Facebook to readily and rapidly recruit new members, establish dates, share experiences, arrange logistics, identify and publicize targets—activities that only two decades ago would have demanded much more time and money. Digital technologies also allow demonstrators not only to maintain close contact throughout the event, but also to react quickly and effectively to shifting police tactics. This enhanced ability to arrange and coordinate protests without the need for a central command, a clearly defined leadership, a large bureaucracy, and significant financial resources has added an entirely new dimension to the nature of political demonstrations.

To summarize, then, justice globalism translates the global imaginary into a concrete political program reflected in the following nine policy demands:

1. A global 'Marshall Plan' that includes a blanket forgiveness of all Third World Debt;
2. Levying of the so-called 'Tobin Tax': a tax on international financial transactions that would benefit the global South;
3. Abolition of offshore financial centres that offer tax havens for wealthy individuals and corporations;
4. Implementation of stringent global environmental agreements;
5. Implementation of a more equitable global development agenda;

6. Establishment of a new world development institution financed largely by the global North through a Tobin Tax and administered largely by the global South;
7. Establishment of international labour protection standards, perhaps as clauses of a profoundly reformed WTO;
8. Greater transparency and accountability provided to citizens by national governments and international institutions;
9. Making all governance of globalization explicitly gender sensitive.

Religious globalisms

Justice globalists were preparing for a new wave of demonstrations against the IMF and World Bank, when, on 11 September 2001, three hijacked commercial airliners hit, in short succession, the World Trade Center in New York and the Department of Defense's Pentagon Building in Washington, DC. A fourth plane crashed in Pennsylvania before the hijackers were able to reach their intended target, most likely the White House. Nearly 3,000 innocent people perished in less than two hours, including hundreds of heroic New York police and firefighters trapped in the collapsing towers of the World Trade Center (see Illustration 13). In the weeks following the attacks, it became clear that the operation had been planned and executed years in advance by the Al Qaeda terrorist network.

Al Qaeda is but one extreme example of organizations that subscribe to various forms of religious globalism. Other religiously inspired visions of global political community include some fundamentalist Christian groups such as the Army of God and Christian Identity, the Falun Gong sect in China, and the Aum Shinrikyo cult in Japan. Despite their deep conservatism, religious globalisms also promote an alternative global vision. This is not to suggest that *all* religiously inspired visions of global community are conservative and reactionary. Indeed, most religions incorporate a sense of a global community united along religious lines, although in general this

13. The burning twin towers of the World Trade Center moments before their collapse on 11 September 2001

is largely informal. A key point about the religious globalist visions, however, is that these groups desire for their version of a global religious community to be all-encompassing, to be given primacy and superiority over state-based and secular political structures. In some cases, they are prepared to use violent means to achieve this end goal.

Indeed, 'jihadist Islamism'—represented by such groups as Al Qaeda, Jemaah Islamiya, Hamas, and Hezbollah—is today's most spectacular manifestation of religious globalism. It feeds on a common perception in the Muslim world that Western modes of modernization have not only failed to put an end to widespread poverty in the region, but that they have also enhanced political instability and strengthened secular tendencies. Thus, jihadist Islamism is a response to what is often experienced as a materialistic assault by the liberal or secular world.

Drawing on revivalist themes popularized in the 18th century by theologian Muhammad ibn Abd al-Wahhab, jihadist Islamists seek to globalize a 'pure' and 'authentic' form of Islam—by any means necessary. Their enemies are not merely the American-led forces of market globalism, but also those domestic groups who have accepted these alien influences and imposed them on Muslim peoples. Jihadists like Osama bin Laden left no doubt that the men linked to his organization committed the atrocities of 9/11 in response to the perceived 'Americanization' of the world: the expansion of the American military around the globe, especially the presence of US military bases in Saudi Arabia; the internationalization of the 1991 Gulf War; the escalation of the Palestinian-Israeli conflict; the 'paganism', 'secularism', and 'materialism' of American-led market globalism; and the eighty-year history of 'humiliation and disgrace' perpetrated against the global *umma* (Islamic community of believers) by a sinister global 'Judeo-Crusader alliance'.

Clearly, it would be a mistake to equate jihadist Islamism of the Al Qaeda variety with the religion of Islam or even more peaceful strands of 'political Islam' or 'Islamist fundamentalism'. Rather, the term 'jihadist Islamism' is meant to apply to those extremely violent strains of Islam-influenced ideologies that articulate the global imaginary into concrete political agendas and terrorist strategies to be applied worldwide. Even after the killing of Osama bin Laden by US Navy SEALs in Pakistan on 2 May 2011, jihadist Islamism Al Qaeda-style is the most influential and successful attempt yet to

Osama bin Laden on *jihad* and America

And the West's notion that Islam is a religion of *jihad* and enmity toward the religions of the infidels and the infidels themselves is an accurate and true depiction.... For it is, in fact, part of our religion to impose our particular beliefs on others.... Their [moderate Muslims] reluctance in acknowledging that offensive *jihad* is one of the exclusive traits of our religion demonstrates nothing but defeat. (2003)

For example, Al Qaeda spent $500,000 on the September 11 attacks, while America lost more than $500 billion, at the lowest estimate, in the event and its aftermath. That makes a million American dollars for every Al Qaeda dollar, by the grace of God Almighty. This is in addition to the fact that it lost an enormous number of jobs—and for the federal deficit, it made record losses, estimated at over a trillion dollars. Still more serious for America was the fact that the *mujahideen* forced Bush to resort to an emergency budget in order to continue fighting in Afghanistan and Iraq. This shows the success of our plan to bleed America to the point of bankruptcy, with God's will. (2004)

I tell you [Americans] that the war [on terror] will be either ours or yours. If it is the former, it will mean your loss and your shame forever—and the winds are blowing in this direction, by Allah's grace. But if it is the latter, then read history, for we are a people who do not stand for injustice, and we strive for vengeance all days of our lives. And the days and nights will not pass until we avenge ourselves as we did on September 11. (2006)

articulate the rising global imaginary into a religious globalism anchored in the core concepts of *umma* and *jihad* (armed or unarmed struggle against unbelief purely for the sake of God and his *umma*).

Indeed, jihadist Islamists understand the '*umma*' as a single community of believers united in their belief in the one and only God. Expressing a populist yearning for strong leaders who set things right by fighting alien invaders and corrupt Islamic elites, they claim to return power back to the 'Muslim masses' and restore the *umma* to its earlier glory. In their view, the process of regeneration must start with a small but dedicated vanguard willing to sacrifice their lives as martyrs to the holy cause of awakening people to their religious duties—not just in traditionally Islamic countries, but wherever members of the *umma* yearn for the establishment of God's rule on earth. With a third of the world's Muslims living today as minorities in non-Islamic countries, jihadist Islamists regard the restoration as no longer a local, national, or even regional event. Rather, it requires a concerted *global* effort spearheaded by jihadists operating in various localities around the world.

Thus, Al Qaeda's desired Islamization of modernity takes place in a global space emancipated from the confining territoriality of 'Egypt', or the 'Middle East' that used to constitute the political framework of religious nationalists fighting modern secular regimes in the twentieth century. Although Al Qaeda embraces the Manichean dualism of a 'clash of civilizations' between its imagined *umma* and 'global unbelief', its globalist ideology clearly transcends clear-cut civilizational fault lines. Its desire for the restoration of a transnational *umma* attests to the globalization of the Muslim world just as much as it reflects the Islamization of the West. Constructed in the ideational transition from the national to the global imaginary, jihadist Islamism still retains potent metaphors that resonate with people's national or even tribal solidarities. And yet, its focus is firmly on the global as jihadist Islamists have successfully redirected militant Islamism's struggle from the traditional 'Near Enemy' (secular-nationalist Middle Eastern regimes) to the 'Far Enemy' (the globalizing West).

Al Qaeda's core ideological claim—to rebuild a unified global *umma* through global *jihad* against global unbelief—resonates well with the dynamics of a globalizing world. It holds special appeal for Muslim youths between the ages of fifteen and thirty who have lived for sustained periods of time in the individualized and deculturated environments of Westernized Islam. This 'second wave' of jihadist recruits, responsible for the most spectacular terrorist operations like the 9/11 attacks or the London bombings of 7/7 (2005), were products of a Westernized Islam. Most of them resided in Europe or North Africa and had few or no links to traditional Middle East political parties. Their enthusiasm for the establishment of a transnational *umma* by means of *jihad* made them prime candidates for recruitment. These young men followed in the footsteps of Al Qaeda's 'first-wavers' in Afghanistan in the 1980s who developed their ideological outlook among a multinational band of idealistic *mujahideen* bent on bringing down the 'godless' Soviet empire.

Their extremist rhetoric notwithstanding, jihadist Islamists like bin Laden's successor Ayman al-Zawahiri never lose sight of the fact that jihadist globalists are fighting a steep uphill battle against the forces of market globalism. They emphasize the ability of American media imperialism to seduce the Muslim world with its consumerist message. They also make frequent references to a continuing and biased campaign waged against the Muslim world by the corporate media—especially 'Hollywood'—for the purpose of misrepresenting Islam and hiding the alleged failures of the Western democratic system.

And yet, even against seemingly overwhelming military odds that translated into a significant weakening of the Al Qaeda network over the last decade, jihadist leaders express their confidence in the ultimate triumph of their vision over 'American Empire'. Despite its chilling and violent content, this vision contains an ideological alternative to market globalism and justice globalism that nonetheless imagines community in unambiguously global terms.

Chapter 8
Global crises and the future of globalization

No doubt, the decade following 9/11 gave an unexpected jolt to the struggle over the meaning and the direction of globalization. As US President George W. Bush made clear time and again, his 'global war on terror' was bound to be a lengthy conflict of global proportions. Against all expectations, the first term of his successor Barack Obama saw as much continuity as change in this regard. Although President Obama removed the last remaining troops from Iraq in December 2011, he failed to close down the infamous military prison at the Guantanamo Bay Naval Base that still houses nearly 200 alleged 'unlawful combatants' in violation of international law. He also continued the 'war of the willing' in Afghanistan, but made clear that his administration was no longer engaged in a global war against a tactic—terrorism—but against Al Qaeda and its terrorist affiliates. But what seemed to worry the charismatic US President more than terrorism were the lingering effects of the Global Financial Crisis (GFC) as the US, Europe, and many countries around the world remained mired in enormous budgetary problems, high unemployment, and anaemic economic growth.

As we noted in previous chapters, however, the GFC is not the only crisis of global proportions that is stalking our interdependent world of the 21st century. Across political, economic, and cultural dimensions, the expansion and intensification of social relations across world-space and world-time has both generated and responded to new 'global crises' beyond the reach of the nation-state and its affiliated political institutions. In addition to worldwide financial volatility and transnational terrorism, these new challenges include climate change and environmental degradation; increasing food scarcity; pandemics such as AIDS, SARS, and H1N1; threats to cyber-security; widening disparities in wealth and wellbeing; increasing migratory pressures; and manifold cultural and religious conflicts. Moreover, the remarkable new wave of popular demonstrations and mass protests (see Illustration 14) cresting in the Arab world and elsewhere might succeed in toppling entrenched undemocratic regimes, but it also has the potential to lead to savage civil wars or condemn vast regions to long-term social and political instability.

This raises the final question we will consider in our examination of globalization: Will these global crises eventually contribute to more extensive forms of international cooperation and interdependence, or might they stop the powerful momentum of globalization?

On first thought, it seems highly implausible that even a protracted GFC or European debt crisis could stop, or even slow down, such a powerful set of social processes as globalization. In fact, the recent emergence of the Group of Twenty (G20) (see Illustration 15) as a rather effective deliberative body with the ability to design and coordinate action on a global scale suggests that perhaps the solution to our global problems is not less but more (and better forms of) globalization.

On the other hand, a close look at modern history reveals that large and lasting social crises often lead to the rise of extremist political groups. The large-scale violence they unleashed proved capable of stopping and even reversing previous globalization trends.

14. **Hundreds of thousands of protestors at Cairo's Tahrir Square, 20 April 2012**

As we noted in Chapter 2, the period from 1860 to 1914 constituted an earlier phase of globalization, characterized by the expansion of transportation and communication networks, the rapid growth of international trade, and a huge flow of capital. Great Britain, then the most dominant of the world's 'Great Powers', sought to spread its political system and cultural values across the globe much in the same way the United States does today. But this earlier period of globalization was openly imperialistic in character, involving the transfer of resources from the colonized global South in exchange for European manufactures. Liberalism, Great Britain's chief ideology, translated a national, not a global, imaginary into concrete political programmes. In the end, these sustained efforts to engineer an 'inter-national' market under the auspices of the British Empire resulted in a severe backlash that culminated in the outbreak of the Great War in 1914.

15. US President Barack Obama with German Chancellor Angela Merkel and Australian Prime Minister Julia Gillard at the G20 Summit in Los Cabos, Mexico, 19 June 2012

In an enduring study on this subject, the late political economist Karl Polanyi locates the origins of the social crises that gripped the world during the first half of the 20th century in ill-conceived efforts to liberalize and globalize markets. Commercial interests came to dominate society by means of a ruthless market logic that effectively disconnected people's economic activities from their social relations. The competitive rules of the free market destroyed complex social relations of mutual obligation and undermined deep-seated norms and values such as civic engagement, reciprocity, and redistribution. As large segments of the population found themselves without an adequate system of social security and communal support, they resorted to radical measures to protect themselves against market globalization.

Polanyi notes these European movements against unfettered capitalism eventually gave birth to political parties that forced the passage of protective social legislation on the national level. After a prolonged period of severe economic dislocation following the end of the Great War, such national-protectionist impulses experienced their most extreme manifestations in Italian fascism and German Nazism. In the end, the liberal dream of subordinating all nation-states to the requirements of the free market had generated an equally extreme counter-movement that turned markets into mere appendices of the totalitarian state.

The applicability of Polanyi's analysis to the current situation seems obvious. Like its 19th-century predecessor, today's version of market globalism also represents a gigantic experiment in unleashing economic deregulation and a culture of consumerism on the entire world. Like 19th-century Britain, the United States is the dominant cheerleader of neoliberalism and thus draws both admiration and contempt from less developed regions in the world. And those who find themselves to be oppressed and exploited by a global logic of economic integration led by an 'American Empire' tend to blame the hegemon for both the emergence and persistence of global crises.

Hence, the United States—together with China, India, Russia, Brazil, and other rising powers—has a special responsibility to search for new and alternative ways of dealing with problems such as the precarious state of the world economy and the natural environment of our beleaguered planet. Only a decade ago, in the wake of the first powerful justice-globalist demonstrations, representatives of the wealthy countries assured audiences worldwide that they would be willing to reform the global economic architecture in the direction of greater transparency and accountability. Yet, even in the wake of the most serious economic crisis since the Great Depression, little progress has been made to honour these commitments and consider justice-globalist alternatives to market-globalist business-as-usual.

This questionable strategy of reacting to global crises by fortifying the market-globalist paradigm with a new rhetoric of mild reformism might work for a relatively short period. But in the long run, the growth of global inequality and the persistence of social instability harbours the potential to unleash reactionary social forces—both communist and fascist—that dwarf even those responsible for the suffering of millions during the 1930s and 1940s. In order to prevent the escalation of violent confrontations between market globalism and its ideological opponents on the Left and Right, world leaders must design and implement a comprehensive Global New Deal that builds and extends genuine networks of solidarity around the world.

Without question, the years and decades ahead will bring new crises and further challenges. Humanity has reached yet another critical juncture—the most important in the relatively short existence of our species. Unless we are willing to let global problems fester to the point where violence and intolerance appear to be the only realistic ways of confronting our unevenly integrating world, we must link the future course of globalization to a profoundly reformist agenda. As I have emphasized in the Preface of this book, there is nothing wrong with greater manifestations of social interdependence that emerge as a result of globalization. However, these transformative social processes must have a moral compass and an ethical polestar guiding our collective efforts: the building of a truly democratic and egalitarian global order that protects universal human rights without destroying the cultural diversity that is the lifeblood of human evolution.

References

There is a great deal of academic literature on globalization, but many of these books are not easily accessible to those who are just setting out to acquire some knowledge of the subject. However, readers who have already digested the present volume may find it easier to approach some of the academic works listed below. While these books do not exhaust the long list of publications on the subject, they nonetheless represent what I consider to be the most appropriate sources for further reading. Indeed, some of them have influenced the arguments made in the present volume. Following the overall organization of this book series, however, I have kept direct quotations to a minimum. Still, I wish to acknowledge my intellectual debt to the authors below, whose influence on this book is not always obvious from the text.

Chapter 1: Globalization: a contested concept

Accessible academic books and texts on globalization published in recent years include: Jan Aart Scholte, *Globalization*, 2nd edn. (St. Martin's Press, 2005); Saskia Sassen, *A Sociology of Globalization* (Norton, 2007); Manfred B. Steger, *Globalisms: The Great Ideological Struggle of the 21st Century* (Rowman & Littlefield, 2009); and Dani Rodrik, *The Globalization Paradox* (Norton, 2011).

For representative collections of influential essays and excerpts on globalization, see George Ritzer (ed.), *The Blackwell Companion to Globalization* (Blackwell, 2007); Manfred B. Steger (ed.), *Globalization: The Greatest Hits: A Global Studies Reader* (Oxford

University Press, 2010); and Frank J. Lechner and John Boli (eds.), *The Globalization Reader* 4th edn. (Wiley Blackwell, 2011). Manuel Castells' *Communication Power* (Oxford University Press, 2011) maps the contours of today's 'global network society'. David Held and Anthony McGrew's anthology, *Globalization Theory* (Polity, 2007), also provides a clear elucidation of leading theoretical approaches to understanding globalization.

There are now several excellent academic journals dedicated to the study of globalization. Some of the most influential include: *Globalizations*, *Global Networks*, *New Global Studies*, *Journal of Critical Globalisation Studies*, and *Global Change, Peace & Security*.

Information on the 2010 World Cup used in this chapter can be gleaned from the following Internet sources: <http://www.fifa.com/worldcup/archive/southafrica2010/>; <http://www.knowyourmoney.co.uk/the-economics-of-the-world-cup/>.

I am especially grateful to Professor Debora Halbert, University of Hawai'i-Manoa, for drawing my attention to the global-local genealogy of the song *Waka Waka* performed by Shakira at the 2010 World Cup. Professor Leo McCann, Manchester Business School, also provided valuable feedback on this section. Biographical information about Shakira can be found on her official website: <http://shakira.com>.

The parable of the blind scholars and the elephant most likely originated in the Pali Buddhist Udana, a collection of Buddhist stories compiled in the 2nd century BCE. The many versions of the parable spread to other religions as well, especially to Hinduism and Islam. I want to thank Professor Ramdas Lamb from the University of Hawai'i for sharing his understanding of the story.

Chapter 2: Globalization and history: is globalization a new phenomenon?

My discussion in the early part of this chapter has greatly benefited from the arguments made by Jared Diamond in his Pulitzer-prize-winning book, *Guns, Germs, and Steel* (Norton, 1999). I also recommend the delightful and very readable histories of globalization assembled by Nayan Chandra, *Bound Together: How Traders, Preachers, Adventurers, and Warriors Shaped Globalization* (Yale

University Press, 2007); Alex MacGillivray, *A Brief History of Globalization: The Untold Story of our Incredible Shrinking Planet* (Running Press, 2006); and Robert McNeill and William H. McNeill, *The Human Web* (Norton 2003).

Some of the essential books surveying the growing field of global history include: A. G. Hopkins (ed.), *Global History* (Palgrave, 2006); Juergen Osterhammel and Niels P. Petersson, *Globalization: A Short History* (Princeton University Press, 2005); Barry Gills and William Thompson (eds.), *Globalization and Global History* (Routledge, 2006); Bruce Mazlish, *The New Global History* (Routledge, 2006); and Pamela Kyle Crossley, *What is Global History?* (Polity, 2008). Two excellent academic journals on the subject are: *Journal of World History* and *Journal of Global History*.

An accessible account of 'world-system theory' authored by Immanuel Wallerstein can be found in his *World-System Analysis: An Introduction* (Duke University Press, 2004). A powerful critique of Wallerstein's alleged Eurocentrism is contained in Andre Gunder Frank, *ReORIENT: Global Economy in the Asian Age* (University of California Press, 1998).

Chapter 3: The economic dimension of globalization

Short, accessible treatment of economic globalization is provided by Joseph Stiglitz, *Making Globalization Work* (W. W. Norton, 2007).

More academic accounts include Jeffry A. Frieden, *Global Capitalism: Its Fall and Rise in the Twentieth Century* (W. W. Norton, 2007); Robert Schaefer, *Understanding Globalization* 4th edn. (Rowman & Littlefield, 2009); and David Harvey, *The Enigma of Capital and the Crisis of Capitalism* (Oxford University Press, 2011).

An overview of neoliberalism is provided in Manfred B. Steger and Ravi K. Roy, *Neoliberalism: A Very Short Introduction* (Oxford University Press, 2010).

The best short treatment of the Global Financial Crisis is Robert J. Holton's, *Global Finance* (Routledge, 2012). An readable insider account of the crisis' origins and evolution can be found in Joseph E. Stiglitz, *Freefall: America, Free Markets, and the Sinking of the World*

Economy (Norton, 2010). Carlo Bastasin's, *Saving Europe: How National Politics Nearly Destroyed the Euro* (Brookings Institution Press, 2012) offers an informed perspective on European Debt Crisis.

The findings of the ground-breaking study of TNC networks referred to in this chapter can found in Stefania Vitali, James B. Glattfelder, and Stefano Battiston, 'The Network of Global Corporate Control', *PLoS* One 6.10 (October 2011), pp. 1–6.

The best sources for empirical data on economic globalization are the annual editions of the UN *Human Development Report* (Oxford University Press), and the World Bank's *World Development Report* (Oxford University Press).

Chapter 4: The political dimension of globalization

David Held's seven points describing the Westphalian model can be found in David Held, Anthony McGrew, David Goldblatt, and Jonathan Perraton, *Global Transformations* (Stanford University Press, 1999) pp. 37–8. My own discussion of political globalization has greatly benefited from insights contained in Chapter 1 of this study. Another excellent introduction to political globalization is John Baylis and Steve Smith, *The Globalization of World Politics*, 5th edn. (Oxford University Press, 2011).

For the arguments of hyperglobalizers, see Martin Wolf, *Why Globalization Works* (Yale University Press, 2005); and Kenichi Ohmae, *The End of the Nation-State* (Free Press, 1995). For the position of the globalization sceptics, see John Ralston Saul, *The Collapse of Globalism* (Viking, 2005); and Peter Gowan, *The Global Gamble* (Verso, 1999). Saskia Sassen's important work on territoriality and global cities contains both sceptical and hyperglobalist arguments. See, for example, *Territory, Authority, Rights: From Medieval to Global Assemblages* (Princeton University Press, 2008), and *The Global City: New York, London, Tokyo* (Princeton University Press, 2001).

On the topic of global politics, economics, public policy, and governance, see James H. Mittelman, *Hyperconflict: Globalization and Insecurity* (Stanford University Press, 2010); Jan Aart Scholte, *Building Global Democracy: Civil Society and Accountable Global*

Governance (Cambridge University Press, 2011); and David Williams and Sophie Harman, *Governing the World? The Practice of Global Governance* (Routledge, 2012).

David Held's elements of cosmopolitan democracy are taken from Daniele Archibugi and David Held (eds.), *Cosmopolitan Democracy* (Polity Press, 1995), pp. 96–120.

Chapter 5: The cultural dimension of globalization

For two comprehensive studies on the cultural dimensions of globalization, see Jan Nederveen Pieterse, *Globalization and Culture: Global Melange* 2nd edn. (Rowman and Littlefield, 2008).

For the arguments of pessimistic hyperglobalizers, see Benjamin Barber, *Consumed* (W. W. Norton and Company, 2007). For the arguments of optimistic hyperglobalizers, see Thomas L. Friedman, *The World Is Flat 3.0: A Brief History of the Twenty-First Century* (Picador, 2007). For the arguments of the sceptics, see Arjun Appadurai, *Modernity At Large* (University of Minnesota Press, 1996); and Roland Robertson, *Globalization* (Sage, 1992).

For the role of the media, see Jack Lule, *Globalization and the Media: Global Village of Babel* (Rowman & Littlefield, 2012); and James D. White, *Global Media: Television Revolution in Asia* (Routledge, 2005).
On English as a global language, see Robert McCrum, *Globish: How the English Language Became the World's Language* (W. W. Norton, 2010).

Chapter 6: The ecological dimension of globalization

An accessible yet remarkably comprehensive book on ecological globalization is Peter Christoff and Robyn Eckersley, *Globalization and the Environment* (Rowman & Littlefield, 2013). My arguments in this chapter have greatly benefitted from Peter and Robyn's insights presented in their learned study.

A concise introduction on global climate change that also effectively debunks the myths of the climate change deniers is Orrin H. Pilkey and Keith C. Pilkey (with Mary Edna Fraser), *Global Climate Change: A Primer* (Duke University Press, 2011).

For the Stern Report, see Nicholas Stern, *The Economics of Climate Change: The Stern Review* (Cambridge University Press, 2007).

The 2012 edition of the UN Environment Program's *Global Environmental Outlook* can be found at: <http://www.unep.org/geo/pdfs/geo5/Measuring_progress.pdf>.

Chapter 7: Ideologies of globalization: market globalism, justice globalism, religious globalisms

For a more detailed account of the ideological dimensions of globalization, see Manfred B. Steger, *The Rise of the Global Imaginary: Political Ideologies from the French Revolution to the Global War on Terror* (Oxford University Press, 2009); and *Globalisms: The Great Ideological Struggle of the 21st Century* (Rowman & Littlefield, 2009).

Readable accounts of globalization from a market-globalist perspective include: Jagdish Bhagwati, *In Defense of Globalization* (Oxford University Press, 2007); Daniel Cohen, *Globalization and Its Enemies* (MIT Press, 2007); and Martin Wolf, *Why Globalization Works* (Yale University Press, 2004).

The five justice-globalist claims and information on global justice movement can be found in: Manfred B. Steger, James Goodman, and Erin K. Wilson, *Justice Globalism: Ideology, Crises, Policy* (Sage, 2013); Geoffrey Pleyers, *Alter-Globalization: Becoming Actors in the Global Age* (Polity, 2010); and Jackie Smith and Marina Karides, *Global Democracy in the World Social Forums* (Paradigm, 2007).

An accessible introduction to the evolution and goals of the US Occupy movement can be found in, Writers for the 99 per cent, *Occupying Wall Street: The Inside Story of an Action that Changed America* (OR Books, 2011).

For a thoughtful discussion of the impact of globalization on Islam, see Nevzat Soguk, *Globalization and Islamism: Beyond Fundamentalism* (Rowman & Littlefield, 2011). Two excellent academic treatments of jihadist globalism and its affiliated movements can be found in: Olivier Roy, *Globalized Islam: The Search for the New Ummah*

(Columbia University Press, 2006); and Fawaz A. Gerges, *The Far Enemy: Why Jihad Went Global* (Cambridge University Press, 2005).

The excerpts from Osama bin Laden's speeches and writings are taken from Raymond Ibrahim (ed.), *The Al Qaeda Reader* (Broadway Books, 2007); and Bruce Lawrence (ed.), *Messages to the World: The Statements of Osama bin Laden* (Verso, 2005).

Chapter 8: Global crises and the future of globalization

For the classic discussion of the backlash against globalization in the interwar period, see Karl Polanyi, *The Great Transformation* (Beacon Press, 2001 [1944]).

For a readable discussion of the alleged decline of the US and the rise of the 'rest', especially China, see Fareed Zakaria, *The Post-American World 2.0* (Norton, 2011); and Martin Jacques, *When China Rules the World* 2nd edn. (Penguin, 2012).

Index

A

advertising 33, 77, 78
Afghanistan 44, 128, 130, 131
Al Qaeda 125, 127–31
alter-globalization 104
America, *see* United States
anti-globalization 104, 105–6
Argentina, neoliberalism in 5

B

Barber, Benjamin 76, 82
bin Laden, Osama 127, 128, 130
biodiversity, reduction in 89, 91
Bretton Woods 38, 39, 56
Buchanan, Patrick J. 104, 105, 106
Bush, George H.W. 65
Bush, George W. 50, 98, 128, 131

C

capitalism 1, 9, 39, 40, 43, 65, 77, 82, 120, 135
Castells, Manuel 14
China 2, 4, 20, 22, 24, 25, 28, 41, 42, 53, 55, 58, 64, 69, 89, 97, 98, 111–4, 125, 136
Chomsky, Noam 118
climate change 87, 92, 93, 95–7, 99, 100–2, 119, 132
Cold War 34, 35, 44
colonization and decolonization 9, 34
consumerism 75, 77, 88, 104, 135
contemporary period (from 1980) 35–6, 75
cultural dimension of globalization 74–86, 131

D

debt 44, 45, 49, 50, 53, 57, 58, 119, 123, 124, 132
definition of globalization 9–16, 18
democracy 72–3, 77, 108, 115, 117, 119
developing countries 39, 42, 46, 57, 58, 89, 97, 121
difference and sameness, culture and 73, 75–82

E

early modern period (1500–1750) 28–31

ecological dimensions of globalization 87–102
climate change 87, 92, 93, 95–7, 99, 100–2
emissions, limits on 92, 97, 99
transboundary pollution 87, 91, 92, 95
treaties, list of 96, 98, 101
economic dimension of globalization 37–59, 118
Bretton Woods 38, 39, 56
capitalism 39, 40, 43
Cold War 44
competition 40–2, 46
developing countries, debts of 39, 42, 46, 57, 58
exchange system 38
inequality 118
international economic institutions, role of 37–9, 41, 55
nation-states 53, 65–70, 135
neoliberalism 40
trade and finance, internationalization of 41–7
transnational corporations 37, 41, 46, 53–6
elephant and blind scholars parable 11, 12, 36
Engels, Friedrich 31–3
English language 1, 84
environment, *see* ecological dimensions of globalization
European Community 69, 70
Europe in the early modern and modern period 28–31
exchange system 38

F

farming societies 22
finance and trade, internationalization of 41–7
food crisis 89
Fukuyama, Francis 77, 115
fundamentalism 127
future of globalization 131–7

G

Gates, Bill 43, 91, 107
GATT (General Agreement on Tariffs and Trade) 39
Global civil society 70, 118
Global crises and the future of globalization 131–8
Global Finance Crisis 48–53, 131
global governance, political globalization and 60, 62, 68–73, 105
global imaginary 10, 11, 15, 18, 34, 82, 104, 105, 124, 127–9, 134
globalisms 103–6, 117–25, 127, 128, 130
globality 9–11
glocalization 2, 5, 80
Gore, Al 92
Greenspan, Alan 112

H

Held, David 13, 62, 72
history, globalization and 17–36
contemporary period (from 1980s) 35–6
early modern period (1500–1750) 28–31
modern period (1750–1970) 31–5
prehistoric period (10,000 BCE–3500 BCE) 20–2
premodern period (3500 BCE–1500 BCE) 22–8
Hormats, Robert 111
human geography 114
hunter-gatherers, migration of 20
hybridization 6, 80
hyperglobalizers 61, 65–7, 75–7, 80

I

ideologies of globalization 103–30
immigration and migration 33–4, 67
imperialism 76, 121, 130
India 2–4, 20, 24, 28, 29, 42, 43, 68, 69, 75, 78, 98, 110, 112, 113, 119, 120, 122, 136
industrialization 34
information and communications technology 14, 17, 35; *see also* Internet
international economic institutions, role of 37, 39, 41, 46, 55–9
International Monetary Fund (IMF) 39, 41, 44, 55–8, 125
international organizations 68, 70
Internet 17, 35, 37, 43, 53, 56, 75, 77, 82, 84, 86, 116
Islam 26, 28, 127–30

J

jihadist Islamism 117, 129–30
jihadist globalism 117, 129–30
justice globalism 103–4, 117–24, 130
- Internet, mobile phones and text messaging, use of 124
- market globalism 104, 106–18, 122, 127, 130, 135–6
- neoliberalism, resistance against 119, 121, 122, 135
- protests 117, 120, 122–4

K

Keynes, John Maynard 39

L

labour market, deregulation of 54
labour movements and socialist parties 34
languages, globalization of 75, 83–6
League of Nations 63
liberalization and deregulation 66, 110
localization 15

M

market globalism 104, 106–18, 122, 127, 130, 135–6
- alter-globalization and anti-globalization 104, 106
- consumerism 75, 77, 88, 104, 135
- democracy, spread of 108, 115, 117
- digital divide 115
- future of globalization 108, 130–7
- imperial globalism 120, 130
- jihadist globalism 117, 129–30
- justice globalism 103–4, 117–24, 130
- liberalization 108–12
- neoliberalism 119, 120, 122
- rich and poor countries, gap between 113
- United States 104, 105, 109, 111, 118

Marx, Karl 31–3
McDonaldization 76
media 7, 14, 35, 75, 82–3, 87, 107, 130
mergers 48, 53, 82
migration and immigration 18, 21, 26, 33, 34, 67, 84
modernity 10, 16, 18, 28, 62, 75, 80, 88, 129
modern period 28–35
multilateral organizations and agreements 69
multinational corporations 32, 111

N

Nader, Ralph 118
nationalism 34, 105

national security 67
nation-states 31, 62–70
demise of nation-states 65–8
early modern period 31
economic globalization 66
identity 63
immigration control 67
international cooperation 63, 67, 68
nationalism 63
national security, terrorism and 67
self-determination 62, 63
trade liberalization and deregulation 66
Westphalian model 61–3, 65
neoliberalism 40, 100, 119, 120, 122, 135
NGO, *see* non-governmental organizations (NGO)
Nixon, Richard 39–40
Nokia's role in Finnish economy 56
non-governmental organizations (NGO) 14, 70, 72, 118

O

Obama, Barak 1, 99, 131, 134

P

plague 26
Polanyi, Karl 135
political dimension of globalization 60–73
population growth 88–9
postmodernism 12, 68, 80
prehistoric period (10,000 BCE–3500 BCE) 20–2
premodern period (3500 BCE–1500 BCE) 22–8
processes and conditions 9, 11
protests against globalization 117

R

regional clubs and agencies 69
religion 22, 26, 28, 87, 125, 127, 128
Ricardo, David 40
rich and poor, inequality between 42
Ritzer, George 76
Robertson, Roland 13, 77, 80

S

sameness or difference, culture and 75–82
sceptics 61, 66, 73, 80
Schuman, Robert 69
self-determination 62, 63, 106
September 11, 2001, terrorist attacks on the United States 67, 125, 126, 127, 128, 130
Silk Road 25
Smith, Adam 40
social relations, activities and interdependencies 13–15, 18, 31, 76, 131, 135
Southeast Asian financial crisis 48
Soviet Union 35, 41, 57, 70
Spencer, Herbert 40
Stern, Nicholas 92–3, 96
stock exchanges 43, 47
structural adjustment programmes 57, 58
supranational institutions and associations 70
Sutherland, Peter 112

T

technology 10, 17, 19, 22, 24, 28, 33, 37, 42, 53, 61, 66, 111, 115; *see also* Internet
terrorism 117, 131, 132
Thatcher, Margaret 40, 110
TNCs, *see* transnational corporations (TNCs)
trade and finance, internationalization of 41–7
transboundary pollution 87, 91, 92, 95

transnational corporations (TNCs) 4, 37, 41, 46, 53–6, 82, 106, 111

U

United Nations (UN) 14, 34, 42, 63, 64, 70, 90, 97, 99–102, 113
United States 1, 32–5, 38–9, 43, 49, 57–8, 67, 89, 97–8, 104–5, 109, 111, 118–34
  climate change 87, 92–3, 95–101, 119, 132
  consumerism 75, 77, 88, 104, 135
  culture, Americanization of 1, 76, 77, 80, 127
  environment 58, 88–9, 91–2, 94–7, 118–19, 124, 136
  immigration 33–4
  imperial globalism 76, 130, 134
  income gap 113
  jihadist globalism 117, 127–30
  justice globalism 117–22, 124
  market globalism 104, 106–13, 117–18, 122–3, 127, 130, 135, 136
  modern period (1750–1980) 31, 33
  terrorism 117, 131–2
  Washington Consensus 57, 58

V

videotapes of Osama bin Laden 127–8

W

Wal-Mart 53–5
war 1, 32, 34, 35, 38, 44–5, 57, 63, 65, 127, 128, 131, 134, 135
Washington Consensus 57, 58
Westphalian state 31, 61–3
wheel and writing, invention of the 18, 22–4
Williamson, John 57
Wilson, Woodrow: 'Fourteen Points' 63
World Bank 39, 41, 42, 44, 55–8, 90, 125
World Economic Forum (WEF) 120
World Social Forum (WSF) 14, 120, 121
World Trade Organization (WTO) 39, 41, 55–6, 70, 105, 122–3, 125

Z

Zapatista rebellion against NAFTA in Mexico 121, 122

ONLINE CATALOGUE

A Very Short Introduction

Our online catalogue is designed to make it easy to find your ideal Very Short Introduction. View the entire collection by subject area, watch author videos, read sample chapters, and download reading guides.

http://fds.oup.com/www.oup.co.uk/general/vsi/index.html

INTERNATIONAL RELATIONS

A Very Short Introduction

Paul Wilkinson

Of undoubtable relevance today, in a post-9-11 world of growing political tension and unease, this *Very Short Introduction* covers the topics essential to an understanding of modern international relations. Paul Wilkinson explains the theories and the practice that underlies the subject, and investigates issues ranging from foreign policy, arms control, and terrorism, to the environment and world poverty. He examines the role of organizations such as the United Nations and the European Union, as well as the influence of ethnic and religious movements and terrorist groups which also play a role in shaping the way states and governments interact. This up-to-date book is required reading for those seeking a new perspective to help untangle and decipher international events.

www.oup.com/vsi